FOLKLORE of ESSEX

FOLKLORE of ESSEX

SYLVIA KENT

Cover image: Will Kemp dancing his way from London to Norwich, 1599
Frontispiece: The Mayflower Morris men, with Billericay's Town Crier. Jim Shrubb, 2005

First published 2005
This edition first published 2009
Reprinted 2013

The History Press
The Mill, Brimscombe Port
Stroud, Gloucestershire, GL5 2QG
www.thehistorypress.co.uk

© Sylvia Kent, 2005, 2009

The right of Sylvia Kent to be identified as the Author
of this work has been asserted in accordance with the
Copyrights, Designs and Patents Act 1988.

All rights reserved. No part of this book may be reprinted
or reproduced or utilised in any form or by any electronic,
mechanical or other means, now known or hereafter invented,
including photocopying and recording, or in any
information storage or retrieval system, without the permission in writing
from the Publishers.

British Library Cataloguing in Publication Data.
A catalogue record for this book is available from the British Library.

ISBN 978 0 7524 3677 7

Typesetting and origination by The History Press

Contents

	Acknowledgements	7
	Introduction	8
one	Essex Traditions	12
two	Witch Country	31
three	Calendar Customs	44
four	Cures and Remedies	72
five	Food Lore	88
six	Curiosities	105
seven	Phenomena	123
eight	Telling Tales	137
nine	County Sounds	151
ten	Music and Movement	160
eleven	Legendary Folk	174
	Bibliography	187
	Index	189

Acknowledgements

I am grateful to the many people who have helped me in gathering material and kindly given me permission to use photographs and text, in particular: Norman Gunby; Beryl Masters; Elli Constantatou and Lloyd Simpson at Essex County Council; Chris Brewster, curator of the Cater Museum; the staff at the Great Dunmow, Saffron Walden and Colchester Castle Museums; Robyn Bechelet, editor of *Essex Countryside and Life*; Sue Cubbin, Martin Astell and staff at the Essex Record Office; librarians in the Billericay, Brentwood, Shenfield, Chelmsford and Colchester Libraries; Malcolm Taylor at the English Folk Dance and Song Society; staff at the Folklore Society; Peter Owen; Sheila Bailey; Ken Marsh; Oliver Rowe at the Ford Motor Co.; David Occomore; Tony Kendall; John New and the Essex Folk Association; Revd Keith Lovell; the Essex Storytellers; John Daldry; Michael Ballard and the Maldon Lions Club; Laurie Ford; Merilyn Baldwin; the Colchester Mayoral Office; David Higgleton; and the many other people who have contributed their precious tales of Essex past.

Thanks also to John Murray, publishers of John Betjeman's collected poems, for the quotation from 'A Few Late Chrysanthemums'.

Special thanks are due to Frances Clamp for her generous help. Also to Mary and Martin Bray; Margaret and Colin Powell; Eve and Bob Gladstone; Shirley and Tony Tolliday; and Liz and Don Wallace. My thanks and love to Peter, Sally, Jenny and Barnaby. Every effort has been made to trace the ownership of photographs and to check that the information given in this book is correct. My apologies for any errors or omissions.

Introduction

A Heritage of County Folklore

> Much of history is lore; much lore is history. Often, there is no certainty about which is which or where one ends and the other takes up the tale.
>
> Alan Bignell

Many books have been written about historical Essex, extolling the virtues of the county's famous people, its contrasting countryside and its coasts that have endured invasions of Romans, Saxons, Vikings and Normans. However, very little space has been given to the folklore and customs of our large county.

What is folklore? The *Oxford English Dictionary* defines folklore as the 'traditional beliefs, customs, songs and stories, preserved in oral tradition among people; the branch of knowledge that deals with these. Popular fantasy or belief'. Other reference sources widen the genre to include witchcraft, food, folk dance, astrology, magic, superstitions, herbal remedies, mythology, legends and ghost stories. Possibly no one phrase can do justice to this overarching subject.

To some, folklore conjures up simple but colourful images of morris men dancing on the village green. Others think of the May queen and her retinue resplendent at the school fête during May Day revels. Folklore is not necessarily a relic of the past; like history, it is always with us. Even the most sophisticated modern bride will ensure good luck by having something old, new, borrowed and blue for her trip down the aisle, and the old custom of giving a newborn baby a piece of silver is still recognised in parts of Essex. There has been a resurgence during the last few years in the traditional use of plants as healing remedies, as handed down by our grandparents. Essex still commemorates major religious Church events such as Christmas, Easter, Pentecost (Whitsuntide) and other calendar festivals. Urban myths are increasing, more so with the advent of the Internet. Workplace superstitions still prevail, despite the sophistication and technology that abounds. Amid modern attitudes, ancient superstitions such as carrying lucky charms, not walking under ladders or just being extra careful on Friday the 13th still influence many people, and old wives' tales are as popular as ever.

The county's dragon tales from ancient times come under the folkloric umbrella and sit alongside rather more modern legends. It is interesting to study the background to the Battle of Maldon, when Byrhtnoth and his warriors defended our Essex shores against the Vikings in AD 991.

Visitors driving into Essex from any direction will immediately recognise the distinctive sign defining our county boundary. The silver seaxes on a red background are repeated in miniature on other town and village signs. I am indebted to Revd Keith Lovell for allowing me to use some illustrations from his *History Through Essex Town and Village Signs* series. The seaxes prominently displayed on our county coat

The coat of arms of Essex County Council.

Galleywood village sign.

of arms were officially granted by the College of Arms on 15 July 1932 and are described as:

> Gules [red], three Seaxes fessewise [side by side, in lengthwise] in pale [down centre of shield] argent [silver], pomels and hilts or [gold], points to the sinister [to the shield carrier's left], and cutting edges upwards.

These weapons are woven into our folkloric history and were probably in use from the early days of the Saxon conquest. No one can say why Essex adopted the seaxes for its symbol, which was in use long before the official grant was made. Some writers suggest that the weapons were chosen because they are a pun on the name of the county, which was called *Eastseaxe* in the *Anglo-Saxon Chronicle*.

Essex has been home to some of the world's leading musicians, writers, painters and inventors, and numerous other distinguished people. There seems to be truth in the old philosophy that in places where the great have dwelt, something impalpable lingers in the dust, so mention is made of some of the legendary folk connected with our county. Old King Cole, of nursery rhyme fame, is there,

Feering village sign.

alongside that brave queen of the Iceni tribe, Boudica, who annihilated the Romans at Colchester in AD 61. Also included are John Ray of Black Notley (1627-1705), who produced the world's first flora of the British Isles; Dr Thomas Barnado (1845-1905), the benefactor who founded the Barkingside refuge for deprived and orphaned children; and Guglielmo Marconi, the physicist and inventor who brought the magic of wireless to the world from the small village of Writtle, near Chelmsford.

Every region has its own special folklore but that of Essex is particularly rich in its traditions, tales and legends. One of its admirers, the late Sir John Betjeman, expressed his enjoyment of our countryside in his lovely poem, 'A Few Late Chrysanthemums', written in 1954:

> The deepest Essex few explore
> Where steepest thatch is sunk in flowers
> And out of elm and sycamore
> Rise flinty fifteenth-century towers.

ONE

Essex Traditions

The Dunmow Flitch

He that repents him not of his marriage in a year and a day either sleeping or waking, may lawfully go to Dunmow and fetch a gammon of bacon.

Sir William Dugdale

For more than 900 years, the people of Great Dunmow have been wedded to the tradition of celebrating one of Britain's oldest folk ceremonies – the Flitch Trials. Brave couples put their marriage on trial and enter the witness box, claiming that they have 'not wished themselves unwed for a year and a day'. The couple who convince the counsel and jury – which consists of six maidens and six bachelors from Dunmow – of their love can claim the coveted flitch of bacon. The word 'flitch' comes from the Old English *flicce* and means 'a salted and cured side of bacon'.

The origin of the Dunmow Flitch Trials remains obscure. There are several versions of the flitch tale; the one which is most often quoted was created in 1854 by the writer William Harrison Ainsworth in his book *The Flitch of Bacon* and his poem 'The Custom of Dunmow', which describes how Sir Reginald FitzWalter (sometimes referred to as Robert) and his wife, disguised as humble folk, present themselves at Little Dunmow Priory, asking for the prior's blessing on their year-old marriage. Reginald says:

> In peasant guise my love I won
> Nor knew she whom she wedded;
> In peasant cot our truth we tried,
> And no disunion dreaded,
> Twelve months' assurance proves our faith
> On firmest base is stead.

So impressed is the prior that he orders the convent cook to present a flitch of bacon to the lovers. The couple then reveal their identity and give lands to the priory on condition that a flitch should be given to any couple who are prepared to make an oath that they had not repented of their marriage for a whole year.

The earliest mention of the Dunmow Flitch tradition occurs in William Langland's *The Vision of Piers Plowman*. Langland was alive during the period 1330-1400. Geoffrey Chaucer also mentioned the tradition in a matter-of-fact way in his Prologue to the *Wife of Bath's Tale*:

> The bacoun was nat fet for hem, I trowe,
> That som men han in Essex at Dunmowe.

There are other literary mentions, including an eighteenth-century ballad opera by Henry Bate, which was produced in 1778 at the Haymarket Theatre under the title of *The Flitch of Bacon*. One of the songs from the opera describes the winning of the flitch:

> Since a year and a day
> Have in love roll'd away
> And an oath of that love has been taken,
> On the sharp pointed stones,
> With your bare marrow bones,
> You have won our fam'd Priory bacon.

Recorded instances of successful claimants of the flitch are few and far between – the first four were in 1445, 1467, 1510 and 1701. The 1701 occasion was the first time that wives were mentioned as having a part to play and also the first time that a formally constituted jury heard the case. After 1751, the custom appears to have lapsed until William Harrison Ainsworth's book, *The Flitch of Bacon*, published in 1854, gave the event tremendous publicity. This resulted in the revival of the Flitch Trials the following year and they have continued to the present time.

The modern version of the pageant is staged every leap year and attracts worldwide television and radio coverage. Included in the 2004 'court' were Judge Michael Chapman, Leading Counsel Claire Rayner OBE, Daniel Pitt, Mary Bard, Chris Hancock QC and Junior Counsel Dave Monk from BBC Essex. The Court Chaplain was Revd Canon David Ainge.

Talberds Ley is where it all happens, with a large marquee to accommodate the crowds who come to listen to the couples talking of their marriages and being subjected to cross-questioning from a bewigged counsel for the bacon and another arguing for the couple. The Flitch Judge presides over the trial to make sure there is fair play. The jury listens carefully to what has been said and then leaves the marquee to decide on the verdict.

Afterwards, the winning couple (although there are usually several couples) are carried from the trials in an ancient chair. The procession, led by men carrying the flitch of bacon, makes its way to the old town hall in Market Place. There, the couple are required to kneel and repeat the flitch oath first used in 1751:

> You shall swear by the Custom of Confession
> That you ne'er made Nuptial Transgression
> Since you were married Man and Wife
> By Household Brawls or Contentious Strife
> Or otherwise in Bed or at Board
> Offended each other in Deed or in Word
> Or since the Parish Clerk said Amen
> Wished yourselves unmarried Agen
> Or in Twelve Month and a day
> Repented not in thought any way
> But continued true and in desire
> As when you joined hands in Holy Quire
> If to these Conditions without all fear
> Of your own Accord you will freely Swear
> A Gammon of Bacon you shall receive
> And bear it hence with Love and good Leave
> For this is our Custom at Dunmow well known
> Though the Sport be ours, the Bacon's your own

The famous chair that carries the winning couple in celebration is kept in the Great Dunmow Museum between Flitch Trials. One of the first Flitch Chairs, made from part of a thirteenth-century stall, is kept at St Mary's church in nearby Little Dunmow.

The Fairlop Fair

> To Hainault Forest Queen Anne she did ride
> And beheld the beautiful oak by her side
> And after viewing it from the bottom to the top
> She said to her court 'It is a Fair-lop'

Hainault Forest, once a regular haunt of highwaymen, became famous in the eighteenth century for an entirely different reason: a large fair which was attended by thousands of people at the height of its popularity. The fair was founded by a successful, if slightly eccentric, ship's pump and block maker from Wapping, Daniel Day, known to his friends as Good Day, reflecting the man's amiable disposition.

Dunmow Flitch. Two sets of claimants with counsel, 1897.

Dunmow Flitch. Mr and Mrs Baalham, one of the winning couples, 2004.

Above left: Dunmow Flitch. Claire Rayner OBE, one of court's counsel.

Above right: Dunmow Flitch. Counsel Daniel Pitt and Dave Monk.

Left: Dunmow Flitch. The flitch of bacon.

Above: Dunmow Flitch. The jury of six maidens and six bachelors.

Right: Dunmow Flitch. One of the chair carriers.

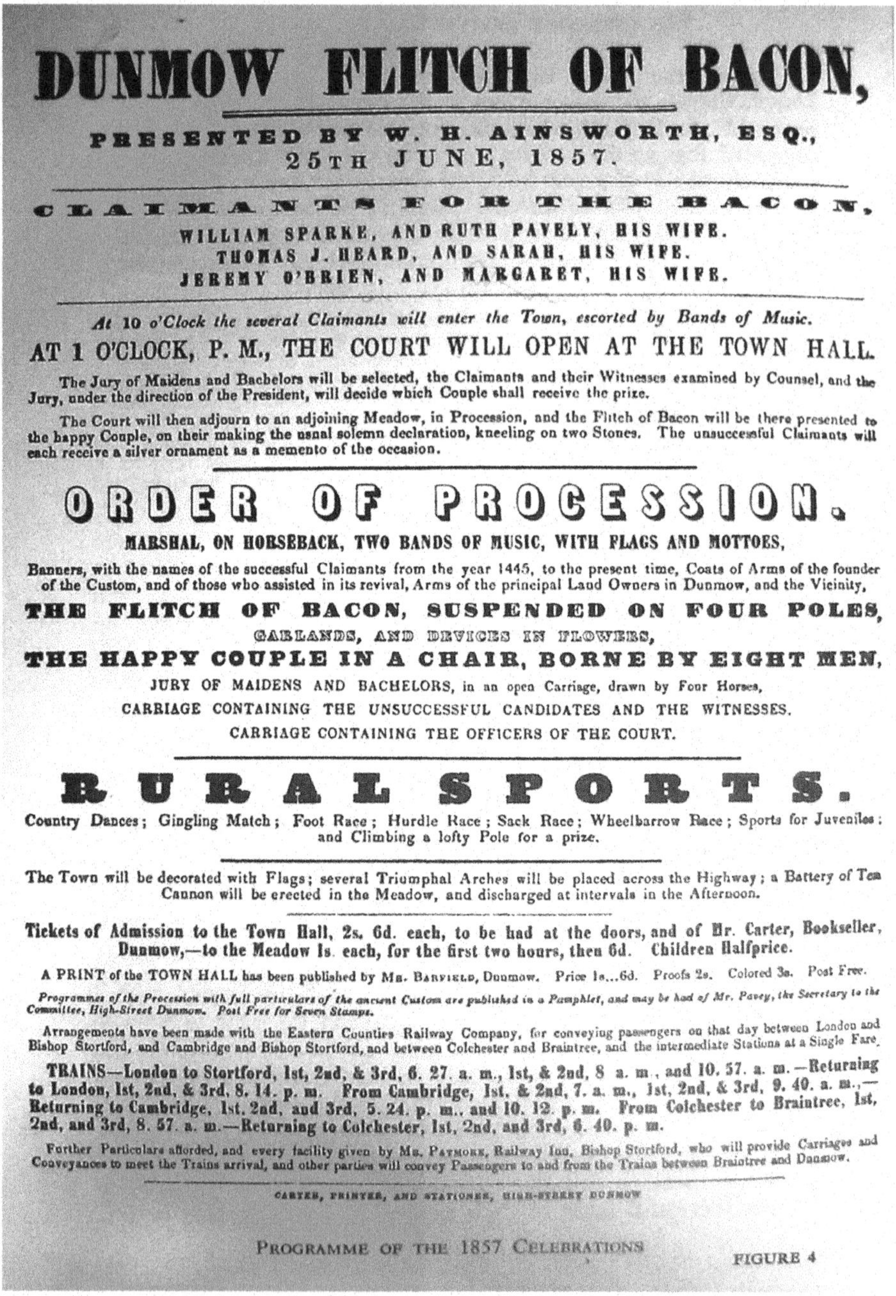

DUNMOW FLITCH OF BACON,

PRESENTED BY W. H. AINSWORTH, ESQ.,
25TH JUNE, 1857.

CLAIMANTS FOR THE BACON,
WILLIAM SPARKE, AND RUTH PAVELY, HIS WIFE.
THOMAS J. HEARD, AND SARAH, HIS WIFE.
JEREMY O'BRIEN, AND MARGARET, HIS WIFE.

At 10 o'Clock the several Claimants will enter the Town, escorted by Bands of Music.

AT 1 O'CLOCK, P. M., THE COURT WILL OPEN AT THE TOWN HALL.

The Jury of Maidens and Bachelors will be selected, the Claimants and their Witnesses examined by Counsel, and the Jury, under the direction of the President, will decide which Couple shall receive the prize.

The Court will then adjourn to an adjoining Meadow, in Procession, and the Flitch of Bacon will be there presented to the happy Couple, on their making the usual solemn declaration, kneeling on two Stones. The unsuccessful Claimants will each receive a silver ornament as a memento of the occasion.

ORDER OF PROCESSION.

MARSHAL, ON HORSEBACK, TWO BANDS OF MUSIC, WITH FLAGS AND MOTTOES,

Banners, with the names of the successful Claimants from the year 1445, to the present time, Coats of Arms of the founder of the Custom, and of those who assisted in its revival, Arms of the principal Land Owners in Dunmow, and the Vicinity,

THE FLITCH OF BACON, SUSPENDED ON FOUR POLES,
GARLANDS, AND DEVICES IN FLOWERS,
THE HAPPY COUPLE IN A CHAIR, BORNE BY EIGHT MEN,
JURY OF MAIDENS AND BACHELORS, in an open Carriage, drawn by Four Horses,
CARRIAGE CONTAINING THE UNSUCCESSFUL CANDIDATES AND THE WITNESSES.
CARRIAGE CONTAINING THE OFFICERS OF THE COURT.

RURAL SPORTS.

Country Dances; Gingling Match; Foot Race; Hurdle Race; Sack Race; Wheelbarrow Race; Sports for Juveniles; and Climbing a lofty Pole for a prize.

The Town will be decorated with Flags; several Triumphal Arches will be placed across the Highway; a Battery of Ten Cannon will be erected in the Meadow, and discharged at intervals in the Afternoon.

Tickets of Admission to the Town Hall, 2s. 6d. each, to be had at the doors, and of Mr. Carter, Bookseller, Dunmow,—to the Meadow 1s. each, for the first two hours, then 6d. Children Halfprice.

A PRINT of the TOWN HALL has been published by Mr. Banfield, Dunmow. Price 1s...6d. Proofs 2s. Colored 3s. Post Free.

Programmes of the Procession with full particulars of the ancient Custom are published in a Pamphlet, and may be had of Mr. Pavey, the Secretary to the Committee, High-Street Dunmow. Post Free for Seven Stamps.

Arrangements have been made with the Eastern Counties Railway Company, for conveying passengers on that day between London and Bishop Stortford, and Cambridge and Bishop Stortford, and between Colchester and Braintree, and the intermediate Stations at a Single Fare.

TRAINS—London to Stortford, 1st, 2nd, & 3rd, 6. 27. a. m., 1st, & 2nd, 8 a. m., and 10. 57. a. m.—Returning to London, 1st, 2nd, & 3rd, 8. 14. p. m. From Cambridge, 1st, & 2nd, 7. a. m., 1st, 2nd, & 3rd, 9. 40. a. m.,—Returning to Cambridge, 1st, 2nd, and 3rd, 5. 24. p. m., and 10. 12. p. m. From Colchester to Braintree, 1st, 2nd, and 3rd, 8. 57. a. m.—Returning to Colchester, 1st, 2nd, and 3rd, 6. 40. p. m.

Further Particulars afforded, and every facility given by Mr. Paymore, Railway Inn, Bishop Stortford, who will provide Carriages and Conveyances to meet the Trains arrival, and other parties will convey Passengers to and from the Trains between Braintree and Dunmow.

CARTER, PRINTER, AND STATIONER, HIGH-STREET DUNMOW.

PROGRAMME OF THE 1857 CELEBRATIONS

FIGURE 4

Dunmow Flitch. 1857 poster advertising the trials.

When collecting rents from tenants who lived in some of his cottages in the Barkingside area, Day decided to treat both his tenants and employees to a picnic – a beanfeast – in the woods. The finest ale, bacon and beans were distributed from the hollow trunk of possibly England's largest oak tree, its trunk measuring 36ft in girth and its seventeen branches extending 300ft in circumference.

Setting out early from the East End on the first Friday in July one year in the early 1700s, Day had made arrangements for the food and ale to be laid out under the old oak. The picnic was a wonderful success and Day decided to repeat it the following July. What had originally started as a private event gradually grew to be an annual festival on the calendar, attracting not only Day's staff and tenants but also the general public. The fair grew in popularity, apparently without causing Day any resentment. In fact, he seemed to enjoy the unexpected expansion.

Day had always had a strong aversion to land travel and chose to travel on water whenever possible. This idiosyncrasy was incorporated into the procession that preceded the fair, which consisted of fully rigged model ships mounted on carriage frames covered with bright awnings, each drawn by six horses with outriders and postillions dressed in blue and gold. The boats were cut out of one piece of fir and each seated thirty or forty 'sailors'. They were called the Fairlop boats. The day of the fair often proved wet, giving rise to a local proverb: 'On Fairlop Friday it will be sure to rain, if only nine drops'.

Vehicles of all kinds followed and musicians escorted the parade. The fair became such a tradition that even Queen Anne, accompanied by her court retinue, paid a visit one summer. When, during one picnic, a branch fell from the old oak, Day saw this as a bad omen and had a carpenter turn the branch into a coffin which he tested for his size and comfort. He died, aged eighty-four, on 19 October 1767, requesting that his body be conveyed to his Barking grave by water, as in life he had met with a number of accidents while travelling over land.

The fair continued after Day's death, and so popular did it become that in 1839, according to missionaries of the Religious Tract Society, there were many sporting events, sideshows, gaming tables and heavy drinking. By this time, the fair had become a three-day event lasting from Friday to Sunday. The following year, there were thousands of revellers in the forest. It is believed that Charles Dickens, as a contemporary journalist, wrote a feature describing the fair in the *Morning Post* in 1854.

By then, however, the venerable oak had gone. Over the years, the surface roots of the tree were damaged by fires lit by the picnickers and revellers, and in 1805 the tree, already suffering from the degradation of time, was seriously damaged by fire. In 1820, the tree, which was by then dead, was finally blown down during a gale. Part of its timber was used by a builder to make a pulpit and reading desk for St Pancras church in Euston Road, London. Despite the loss of its namesake, the Fairlop Oak Festival continued to be held until July 1899.

The Fairlop Oak – the new planting in 1992.

Opposite above: The Fairlop Oak, 1790.

Opposite below: The Fairlop Frigate, from the *Illustrated London News*, 1843.

A replacement for the Fairlop Oak was paid for and planted, on 21 February 1992, on the exact site of the ancient oak by Ilford historian and writer Mr Norman Gunby and the East London Soroptomists.

Colchester's Famous Oyster Feast

Essex oysters are famous throughout the world. They have been cultivated around the Thames Estuary, particularly in Colchester, since before the time of the Roman invasion. The Romans found these succulent shellfish so delicious that they set about establishing an industry around the Colchester beds, even exporting them to Rome. Oysters were also cultivated in other places in the county, including Maldon, Pagelsham, Leigh, Canvey and Southchurch. Celebrations take place in some towns; the most famous is the annual Colchester Oyster Feast.

The Colchester oyster fishery is officially 'opened' on the first Friday of September each year. In full civic regalia, the mayor of Colchester, his town clerk and council members take passage on an oyster dredger out into the Pyefleet Channel of the Colne Estuary, off Mersea Island. A flotilla of small boats carrying invited guests follows the mayor out into the channel. Oaths are sworn, pledging devotion to the Queen, and the mayor dredges and eats the

Colchester Oyster Feast. Colchester's mayor consumes the first oyster.

Colchester Oyster Feast. Invited guests at the Moot Hall, Colchester.

first oyster of the season. Gin and gingerbread follow and then there is an oyster lunch on board.

The grand Colchester Oyster Feast is held on the last Friday of October each year. It takes place at Colchester's Moot Hall and is presided over by the mayor. No one knows when the first Oyster Feast was held but it was an established annual event by the reign of King Charles II. It took place on 9 October, marking the start of the ancient Saint Denys' Fair. This fair dated from 1319 and was the greatest of all fairs in Essex, with festivities taking place over eight days.

In modern times, the Colchester Oyster Feast has grown in size and importance and has been attended by many members of the Royal Family and civic dignitaries from around the nation. The mayor also invites Colchester citizens who are active in local charities, civic bodies and good causes. There is a public lottery to ensure that every citizen of the borough has the chance to attend this prestigious event. The arrival of the oysters is greeted by a fanfare of trumpets, signalling the start of the feast. The Town Clerk reads the proclamation, dating from 1256, which states that the oyster beds have belonged to Colchester 'from the time beyond which memory runneth not to the contrary', and the feast begins.

The Whispering (or Lawless) Court

Until the end of the nineteenth century, an unusual tradition took place annually, around the time of Michaelmas, at Rochford. Following a splendid supper at the King's Head in Rochford marketplace, provided by the lord of the manor, tenants of the town made their way at midnight to congregate around a white-painted wooden post in the front garden of the ancient King's Hill Cottage. The lord's steward whispered the names of the people who owed service to the manor, the tenants replied by whispering their names and the steward concluded with the following proclamation:

> Oh yes, oh yes, oh yes, all persons who have appeared at this court for the manor of King's Hill have leave to depart hence keeping their day and hour on a new summons. God save the King.

This ended the proceedings. The torches were extinguished and the men left. No one knows exactly when this custom started but it is believed to have originated in the mid-seventeenth century, when the second Earl of Warwick was lord of the manor. His tenants were annoyed at his long absences abroad and complained that he was never present to hear their grievances and land disputes. On arriving home late one night after a long journey, he retired to bed but was awoken around midnight by the crowing of a cock that had been startled by the lanterns carried by the tenants in the courtyard below. Believing that that they were

The cottage in Rochford where the Whispering Court took place.

plotting against him, he strode out to meet his men, mistakenly reprimanding them for their treachery. As penance, he commanded them every year thereafter on the Wednesday following Michaelmas Day to assemble around the post to pay homage for their lands – but in hushed voices.

In time, the Whispering Court developed into a boisterous annual event, with the village lads carrying flaming torches and 'crowing' lustily in keeping with the legend, throwing their firebrands into the middle of the marketplace and chanting the 'Song of the Lawless Court'. The beginning of the nineteenth century saw the departure of the manorial lords and with them their courts and other interesting but strange customs. The white-painted wooden post still stands today at King's Hill Cottage, as decreed.

Boy Bishops

The ancient tradition of electing a boy bishop into the local church each year was well known in many places, including Essex, during the Middle Ages. St Nicholas is the patron saint of schoolboys and on his feast day, 6 December, an ordinary chorister was chosen to become 'bishop' for three weeks, until Holy Innocents' Day on 28 December.

During that time, the chosen one was addressed as St Nicholas and treated with reverence by clerics and laymen alike. He was expected to perform most of the duties of an adult prelate. He wore a miniature cope and mitre and carried a crozier, and was assisted by other boys acting as his lesser clergy. He sang Vespers and took a chief part in all the church services, except those which only an ordained priest could celebrate. On his last day as bishop, he was required to preach a sermon and to ride out in procession to bless the people. Henry VIII suppressed this custom in 1541, Mary I revived it in 1554 and Elizabeth I abolished it once more.

During the nineteenth century, the custom was revived in parts of East Anglia. In 1899, Revd H.K. Hudson reintroduced the Boy Bishop ceremony in the small village of Berden, which is not far from Saffron Walden, and it continued annually until he left the village in 1937. Over the last ten years, the custom has become popular again, in a shortened form, in some church schools in Essex.

Seeking Sanctuary

For 1,000 years, the ancient custom of seeking sanctuary, instituted by Pope Boniface V in AD 633, existed in England. This meant that any sinner seeking refuge in a church could remain there safely for up to forty days, free from persecution by his enemies. No doubt the idea was prompted by the Pope's interpretation of the scriptures that decreed that there was 'always room in Heaven for the sinner ready to repent'.

The Thomas à Becket Chapel at Brentwood proved to be a place of sanctuary for Hubert de Burgh, chief minister to King John and later to King Henry III. In 1232, Hubert angered King Henry, who branded him as a traitor and confiscated his home and possessions. Hubert decided to leave Essex and, so great was his haste, it is said he 'had no time to don his clothes'. With armed soldiers in hot pursuit, Hubert sought sanctuary in the chapel at Brentwood, which had been built nine years earlier. But the soldiers ignored Church law and prepared to drag Hubert from the chapel. Hubert stood bravely before the soldiers, his cross in one hand, but this did not prevent the soldiers trying to force the local blacksmith to make shackles to prevent Hubert from escaping. However, when the blacksmith realised the identity of the prisoner, he refused, saying:

> Do with me as you please: as the Lord liveth I will not make shackles for him, but will rather die the worst death there is. Let God judge between you and him for using him so unjustly. Is he not that most faithful and noble-minded Hubert who so often saved England from the ravages of foreigners and restored England to herself?

The Bishop of London, upon hearing that his monarch had violated sanctuary, threatened to excommunicate all involved. As a result, Hubert was returned to

Brentwood Chapel ruins.

the chapel, where he stayed as a prisoner for thirty-nine days. The soldiers then re-arrested him and 'sette him on a sorry horse and conveyed him to the Tower of London'. There was a happy ending, as Hubert was eventually pardoned by the King and had his lands restored. He died in retirement in 1243.

Birthplace of Henry Fitzroy

Henry VIII's relationship with Anne Boleyn and the political consequences of his efforts to produce a male heir are well known in national history. However, little space has been given to Henry's illegitimate son, who was born in the village of Blackmore, where Henry's mistress, Elizabeth Blount, was living.

Young Elizabeth had entered the royal court at an early age, serving as lady-in-waiting to the Queen before catching Henry's eye. She became his mistress a year before giving birth to their son on 18 June 1519. The baby was born at Jericho House, not far from St Laurence's parish church and the Augustinian priory founded in Blackmore at the end of the twelfth century. He was christened Henry Fitzroy, (Fitzroy means 'son of a king'). Elizabeth was married off to one of Cardinal Wolesley's retainers. According to Essex historian Philip Morant, when the King was absent from the court, courtiers would comment that 'he has gone to Jericho'. The nearby river Can was known as 'the Jordan'.

By 1525, it was clear that Queen Catherine would not be able to produce the heir that Henry so desperately needed and young Henry Fitzroy, now his father's pride and joy, was brought out of obscurity and heaped with honours. On his sixth birthday, he became the Duke of Richmond and Somerset and was elected Knight of the Garter, among other prestigious titles.

In the spring of 1532, young Henry came to live at Hatfield in Hertfordshire and, although he was often taken to hunt beside the river Lea, it seems he never returned to live in his native Essex. He died in 1536, aged seventeen, at St James's Palace. The crown on the Blackmore village sign is the only clue to Henry VIII's amorous connections with the area.

St Laurence's Blackmore church

Henry Fitzroy, born in Blackmore on 18 June 1519.

The Victors of Tyler's Common

A story that is now an Upminster legend concerns Tyler's Common. In 1939, just before the Second World War, Essex County Council bought part of the land as the Government pressed every piece of spare land into service to grow food crops. The laborious task of clearing and levelling the overgrown common took months but eventually it was brought into cultivation, although it was not particularly productive and many local people, especially those who had worked hard, felt it was a huge waste of time.

At the end of the war, residents living near the common assumed that the land would revert to its former common land status but officers from Essex County Council erected barbed-wire fences and started offering terms to local farmers for letting the common. When these facts became known, there was considerable indignation from local residents.

It appeared that the stewards of the manor of the common had sold the rights of land, including the common and roadside waste lands along the neighbouring lanes, to Essex County Council for £210 4s 10d. Local farmers were vexed at the proposal to charge them heavily for the use of land which they had always regarded as being theirs by right.

A group of local residents launched an attack on the proposals. Among them was a well-known local man, Edward Luther, who lived at nearby Ardleigh Green. In 1951, he led a well-publicised crusade against the injustice of the Essex County Council's action. He put up posters and drove around the neighbourhood in his small car, liberally daubed with slogans, blasting out the well-known tune 'Colonel Bogey' to attract attention to his cause.

Many people supported Luther, particularly when he put notices on the common threatening those caught stealing the people's common land with trial at Redden Court and, on conviction, hanging by the neck at Gallows Corner. This attracted nationwide attention and photographs of Luther and the Upminster protesters appeared in several national newspapers.

Among the group of local farmers and supporters was the local MP, Mr Geoffrey Bing KC, who, as an authority on common law, was able to dispute the activities of Essex County Council. He provided a legally worded form of petition to Parliament. It required 300 signatures; they were obtained within a day and the petition was presented.

The Luther Stone still stands facing Upminster (Tyler's) Common.

Victory celebrations on Upminster Common, 19 July, 1951.

Accordingly, the Minister for Agriculture announced that it was illegal for any person to fence the common without his consent. As Essex County Council had not sought this consent, they were forced on 19 July 1951 to remove 1¼ miles of wire fencing, much of which had been damaged by protesters. A celebration was held on the common and local farmers drove their cattle on to the common to graze. A victory stone was erected facing the common, which reads:

The Battle of Upminster Common
1 June to 19 July 1951

In the name of King John and the Magna Carta,
this stone is to commemorate
the victory of the commoners
over the Essex County Council

Geoffrey Bing KC MP
Edward A. Luther
Edgar Fordham
Ben Cunningham

TWO

WITCH COUNTRY

> She comes by night in fearsome flight
> In garments black as pitch
> The queen of doom upon her broom
> The wild and wicked witch
>
> Jack Prelutsky

Witchcraft has, it seems, always been with us and is entwined within Essex folklore. Some years ago, one of the country's leading authorities on witchcraft, Eric Maple, wrote: 'A mere broomstick's ride from central London – and an even shorter air hop from Stansted and Southend airports, lies the Essex witch country, an extensive, low-lying area between the River Thames and the River Stour, which separates Essex from Suffolk.'

Many apparently unexceptional Essex towns and villages that are now within London's commuter belt were coloured by a terrifying fear and superstition. Why Essex in particular became the hub of witchcraft activity 300 years ago is uncertain. During Tudor times, Londoners experienced many bouts of plague and sickness. As some curative 'white witchcraft' was believed to be found in some Essex villages – not too far from the capital – many sought relief from the healers and wise women known to live in the county.

Certainly, Essex seems to have been considered the breeding ground for much sorcery and magic from the fifteenth to the eighteenth centuries and, in some places, even well into the nineteenth century. Fear and superstition are the twin preoccupations that seem to have started the awful upsurge of witchcraft mania that swept through Catholic Europe like a tidal wave, eventually arriving in England.

In 1542, Henry VIII declared war on witches by introducing a statute against witchcraft. Almost immediately from that time, poor, simple women began to be

Hanging witches.

persecuted. 'Thou shalt not suffer a witch to live,' was the biblical command. 'A man or also women that hath a familiar spirit, or that is a wizard, shall surely be put to death. They shall stone them with stones; their blood shall be upon them.' With that indictment being promulgated nationally, the die was set, although the Act was repealed five years later when Henry died and his son, the nine-year-old Edward VI, was crowned in Westminster Abbey on 20 February 1547.

During Edward's six-year reign, the *Book of Common Prayer* was introduced and the Act of Uniformity passed two years later, which prohibited the use of the Catholic Mass. Removal from churches of the people's precious statues of the saints and beautiful icons caused much offence in many Essex parishes and, from a religious view, there was great uncertainty and confusion among ordinary village folk.

When Elizabeth became Queen after the death of her half-sister, the devoutly Catholic Queen Mary, the subject of witchcraft was again the talk of Parliament and became the basis of new legislation that entered the Statute Book in 1563. During that year, there was great sickness in London, with more than 17,000 dying of a plague, and in this atmosphere the healing powers of 'white witchcraft' was again sought.

In his book *Broomstick Over Essex*, Tom Gardiner offers some interesting ideas about witchcraft at that time:

Elizabeth came to the throne in 1558 and the Church of England was back in business. John Jewel, now appointed Bishop of Salisbury, was given the honour of preaching before Her Majesty in 1560, and used the occasion to sound the trumpet for persecution. 'Your Grace's subjects pine away to death,' he said, 'their colour fadeth, their flesh rotteth, their speech is benumbed, their senses bereft.'

It is sensational language, guaranteed to inspire the persecutor. Elizabeth knew, of course, that some of her less attractive subjects had the disconcerting pastime of making models of her and sticking pins in them. She also suspected that those embracing another religion, or not wholly on the side of the Church of England, might just be using this as a cover for revolutionary opinions. It was a time when national stability could not be taken for granted and a religious freak might be a disguised political enemy. Perhaps, therefore, she did not take much persuading.

It wasn't until 1563 that witchcraft was made a capital offence. Even then, English law required proof of injury to people or domestic animals. A charge of witchcraft in England led to death by hanging, not burning, as was the case in France and Germany. When Pope Paul VIII issued an edict in 1584 which made witchcraft a heresy, he gave power to the continental Inquisitors to search out and severely punish all witches. The Inquisitors were given elementary and primitive instructions but they soon introduced refinements. A century earlier, two Dominican friars, Heinrich Kramer and Jakob Sprenger, had written a treatise entitled *Malleus Maleficarum* or *The Hammer of Witches*. This textbook was considered to be an extraordinary piece of incredulity and sub-pornography and was compiled at the request of Pope Innocent VII. 'Many persons,' said the Pope's letter, 'unmindful of their own salvation and straying from the Catholic Faith, have abandoned themselves to devil's incubi and succubi.' The treatise became a handbook used for guidance by those in authority when searching out witches.

In England at that time, witchcraft was not considered heresy, and torture was forbidden as a general rule. However, this did not stop many people being persecuted and killed. In Essex alone, around 550 people were accused of witchcraft and around 100 sent to the scaffold between 1560 and 1680. The Assize courts at Chelmsford held the melancholy distinction of having hanged more unfortunate people who had been condemned as witches than any other English county. From court accounts, they were mostly poor, often deranged and generally elderly women, although there were some cases of elderly men being accused. They appear to have been convicted on flimsy evidence that would have been thrown out by many other courts in the country.

To set the scene and attempt to understand the fear of that period, it is necessary to picture Essex as it was in the sixteenth century. The county was dotted with tiny villages standing in lonely spots near some desolate, windswept marsh or salting, or bordering the extensive woodland that covered much of the area in past centuries. The villagers were often uneducated and illiterate. Their very existence hung by a thread: if inclement weather caused a bad harvest, or a cow or pig died, hardship and starvation inevitably followed. Their lack of scientific knowledge made crop failures, unusual illnesses or unseasonable weather conditions something of a mystery. A reasonable explanation was always sought and very often witchcraft was a useful scapegoat.

So it was in Essex and the Eastern Counties that many women – and a few men – were tortured, hanged or drowned by the 'swimming' method, which was in accordance with the ancient belief that water, the element of baptism, would reject a witch. The victim had her right thumb tied to her left big toe and was thrown into the village pond. If the woman sank, she was innocent but if she floated then she was definitely a witch and was condemned to die on the scaffold. No one, it appeared, was safe. Even the 'wise women', who until then had often been respected midwives, possessing knowledge of plant cures for illness using herbs growing in the countryside, were now in danger of being branded a sorceress or witch. Telling fortunes, charming warts or just administering age-old country remedies learned from their parents to cure sick folk and their animals all came within the scope of the witch-watchers.

Glyn Morgan, in his book *Essex Witches*, tells us that the first Chelmsford witch trial took place in 1545. On the opening day, the Revd Thomas Cole, the local rector, and Sir John Fortescue, the Keeper of the Royal Wardrobe, presided but the trial was considered to be of such importance that the Attorney-General, Sir Gilbert Gerard, and a judge of the Queen's Bench, John Southcote, took over. In that first trial, the defendants were three women from Hatfield Peverel: Agnes Waterhouse, her daughter Joan and Elizabeth Francis.

Agnes Waterhouse seems to have been a most unpopular person. She was quarrelsome and had many enemies in the village. While she was awaiting trial at Chelmsford, the sixty-four-year-old confessed to being a witch. She told the court that she had commanded her neighbour's cat, Sathan, to kill one of her pigs. Sathan had a reputation for causing illness and death. Once in Agnes's home, Sathan was apparently instrumental in killing several animals belonging to neighbours who had had a disagreement with Agnes in the past. She rewarded him with a chicken and a drop of blood. No neighbour who had disagreed with her over the years escaped punishment. The details of this first trial have been written into witchcraft history, including the statement that, nine years earlier, having become tired of her husband, Agnes had commanded Sathan to kill him.

Agnes's eighteen-year-old daughter Joan was cross-examined while her mother was in prison and admitted that when she was alone in the house, she had experimented with what she had seen her mother do. She called Sathan, who appeared from under the mother's bed in the guise of a huge dog. She wanted the dog to punish a neighbour who had been unkind to her. Shortly afterwards, this neighbour suddenly saw 'an evyll favoured dogge with hornes on his head', which scared her so much that she was literally paralysed in her right arm and leg. Agnes

Waterhouse was charged with causing death by witchcraft, assisted by her 'familiar' Sathan, and was hanged on 29 July 1566. To her belongs the distinction of being the first of the 'great witches' of the period. Her daughter Joan was found not guilty.

Elizabeth Francis was the third person in court with the Waterhouse women and it was she who was the original owner of the cat Sathan, who was said to be her 'familiar' or imp. She vouched for the efficacy of Sathan's powers, as she had benefited by ridding herself of the baby she was expecting by Andrew Byles, who refused to marry her, and using magic to cause his death. Then, after marrying Christopher Francis, she was also implicated in his death. She commanded Sathan to lame her husband. This the cat did by transforming himself into a toad and jumping into one of Christopher's shoes. The lameness could not be healed and he died soon after from natural causes. This suited Elizabeth, who had not been happy with her husband. When her confession was laid before the court, she was found guilty but, despite having committed two murders and one abortion, she was sentenced to only one year's imprisonment. Thirteen years later, however, Elizabeth was involved in witchcraft once more and this time she was sent to the gallows.

Although there were many Essex villages in the northern part of Essex that were well known for incidents of witchcraft during the sixteenth and seventeenth centuries, there were several areas that had little or no witchcraft activity, such as Stansted Mountfichet, Great and Little Easter, West Bergholt, Marks Tey, Stanway, Ardleigh to Great Bromley and a long line stretching from the Easters

A witch weathervane.

to Hutton. The Benfleet and Thundersley regions also seem to have been fairly quiet. These were perhaps areas of little religious enthusiasm. By contrast, Barking and Dagenham seem to have been lively. It has been suggested that this could have something to do with the far-reaching effects of the strong Catholic traditions of Barking Abbey, which had been suppressed many years earlier after Henry VIII's break from Rome. Tom Gardiner writes:

> Hatfield Peverel, on the other hand, was of some Puritan intensity and I am inclined to think the same went for Brightlingsea, St Osyth, Clacton, the Sokens, indeed virtually the whole of the Tendring Hundred. It is very difficult for us in the twentieth century to appreciate what a regard these people had for religion. It was a burning issue; its language came to their lips quite naturally. Above all, an interest in it said much for the kind of person you were. Adjectives like Catholic and Protestant took in the whole of life; which is why Colchester occupies such a significant place in this period.

Another local case of witchcraft involved several women in St Osyth, one of whom was Grace Thurlowe. Her baby boy had been feverish for some months and she called in one of her neighbours, Ursula Kempe. This woman always went quietly about her business in the remote and quiet village of St Osyth and it would have been difficult to believe that she would become the centre of a notorious witch-hunt. She was known to be knowledgeable about herbs and healing and was particularly good with children. Mother Kempe made three visits. She took the child by its hands and talked to him gently, issuing 'magic words', so the delighted mother said, and the boy's health improved.

Grace worked for the lord of the manor, Mr Brian Darcy, and when she gave birth to another child, a girl, her employer suggested she again seek the help of Mother Kempe with her confinement. Grace refused, suspecting that Mother Kempe's special knowledge had connections with witchcraft. Mother Kempe was offended. A while later, the baby fell out of its cot and was badly injured. In front of neighbours, the old nurse was accused of bewitching the child, a charge that was denied. The baby's condition worsened, so another wise-woman was consulted but she could not lift the so-called curse that Mother Kempe had laid on both mother, who was now suffering from lameness, and child. Previously content to have Mother Kempe use her powers to heal, the citizens of St Osyth now began to lay all the evils of the village at her door.

Small children, who had colourful imaginations, were called to give evidence. Thomas Rabbet, Mother Kempe's eight-year-old son, went into court and declared that his mother had four spirits – Tyffin, Tyttie, Pygine and Iacke. Tittie was a little grey cat, Tyffin a white lamb, Pygine a black toad and Iacke a black cat. He said his mother fed these creatures on beer and white bread and he had seen them suck her blood.

The local magistrates found themselves with what was supposedly a whole coven of local witches. Mother Kempe was charged with five murders and other women in the village were also accused of sorcery offences, resulting in Darcy sending at least ten to the gibbet, including Mother Kempe. In 1921, two skeletons were found in St Osyth while building renovations were taking place. The elbows and knees of the two women's skeletons were riveted through with iron pins, to prevent them walking as 'living dead'.

Familiars

The belief that witches possessed imps, usually in the form of small creatures such as mice and rats, which were believed to have been given to them by the Devil, was one of the most persistent in Essex. These evil spirits or imps were the surest sign of a witch. An outstanding feature of many of the cases that came to court at the time was the number of domestic 'familiars' that were supposed to have played an important part in their mistresses' witchcraft activities.

The witches often had cats, dogs, ferrets and in some cases, toads which were believed to be demons in animal form. These creatures were supposed have assisted the witch in carrying out her malicious acts and the trial records depict them as having incredible, unearthly powers. The familiar was by no means a subservient, faithful helper who followed the witch's every command. The relationship between the familiar and the witch is better characterised as 'give-and-take'. Some familiars were believed to have played the role of devils or imps, in that they requested a pact (often satanic in nature) before they would perform any services for the witch. Furthermore, almost all of them craved nourishment in the form of human blood. They would attach themselves to some part of the witch's body and suck blood out of her, leaving a bruise that witch-hunters called 'the witch's mark'. When the witch purge was at its height, some unfortunates were executed just because they kept animals or had a few moles on their bodies.

King James I

After the awful witch trials in the early years of Elizabeth's reign, the witchcraft craze simmered down. However, in 1594, Essex lawyer William Smith wrote:

> A witch or hag is she which, being eluded by a league made with the devil through his persuasion, inspiration and juggling, thinkest she can design what manner of things soever, either by thought or imprecation, as to shake the air with lightnings and thunder, to cause hail and tempests, to remove green corn or trees to another place, to be carried by her familiar, which hath taken upon him the deceitful shape

of a goat, swin, calf, etc. into some mountain far distant, in a wonderful short space of time. And sometimes fly upon a staff or fork, or some other instrument. And spend all night with her sweetheart, in playing, sporting, banqueting, dalliance and divers other devilish lusts and lewd desports, and to show a thousand such monstrous mockeries.

When Elizabeth died in 1603 and James IV of Scotland ascended the English throne, becoming James I, a new Act regarding witchcraft was placed on the Statute Book. It was far more severe than its predecessors. This came as no surprise since Scottish practice followed continental themes. From that time, death was to be the punishment for any witch committing a second offence.

The Witch-hunters

The sixteenth-century outbreak of witchcraft appears naïve in comparison with the much more terrible terror to come. For a generation, witchcraft in East Anglia seems to have gone underground but in 1644, amid the upheavals of the Civil War,

The Witchfinder General and imps.

Matthew Hopkins, self-styled Witchfinder General.

on to the scene came Matthew Hopkins, the lawyer son of a Suffolk parson who lived at Manningtree.

The *Dictionary of National Biography* states that 'little is known of Hopkins prior to 1644' but there is plenty of documentation and proof of Hopkins' activities as self-styled Witch Finder General. Richard Deacon, in his book *Matthew Hopkins – Witch Finder General*, states:

> From what scant evidence we have it seems probable that Hopkins first knew Mistley and Manningtree as a youth when he worked for a shipping owner at Mistley. Assuming that he was born sometime after 1619 – it is unlikely that it was later than 1622 – he would have been about twenty when he went to Ipswich to work in a lawyer's office or, as seems likelier, in the legal department of some shipping firm. One simply cannot take it for granted, as so many have done, that he had qualified as a solicitor or barrister, for the proof of this does not exist. Yet so many writers have described him as a failed lawyer.

At some time during the early 1640s, Hopkins seems to have made a few influential friends, probably through his work at Mistley, and from 1644 he appears to have assiduously studied books on witchcraft, including King James's book, *Daemonologie*, which he published in 1597, and Thomas Potts' account of the Pendle witches' trial in 1612. He would also have known about and very probably read the depositions of the St Osyth witches' trial in Essex. There is uncertainty about when very first actions against witches were brought by Matthew Hopkins but it was not until July 1645 that Hopkins launched the trial of sixteen women and not until the end of that year that five were found guilty and hanged.

New legal directives were eagerly adopted by Hopkins, with terrifying results. He and his assistants, John Stearn and Mary Phillips, swept through the Eastern Counties like avenging angels. Whenever an informer indicated a witch, Mary examined the suspect for identifying devil marks. If a wart, a pimple or a birthmark was found, the victim was subjected to a ruthless and cruel examination, which usually produced a confession – and led to the victim's death.

So much has been written about Hopkins' reign of terror, yet it was relatively short, lasting from 1644 until the autumn of 1646, when there was a steadily mounting campaign of criticism against Hopkins. Gradually, it came to be realised that more witches were being executed than ever before in the history of England. Hopkins' campaign resulted in the execution of several hundred witches, with many more elderly women dying in prison through the effects of torture.

A great deal of criticism was devoted to the fact that, alongside the power that he enjoyed, Hopkins was also making large amounts of money from his unsavoury activities. Twenty shillings was paid for every witch he discovered, and Mary Phillips and John Stearn also fared well.

The tide was turning against Hopkins, and allegations of corruption and fortune-hunting were being levelled at him and his assistants. In 1647 he wrote a pamphlet, 'The Discoverie of Witches', published later that year, in which he cleverly put forward a series of reasoned arguments in the hope of disarming his critics and impressing local magistrates. But his time was running out. He failed to influence those in power and he disappeared from the scene.

Some accounts say he was himself hanged as a witch; others suggest that he died from consumption in his own bed at Mistley. There was a also a tale that he joined his brother in America under an assumed name. Perhaps one day we may find the answer. Despite the supposedly remarkable success of Hopkins, he failed to eradicate witchcraft from Essex and it is said that it continues to this day.

Cunning Murrell

From 1812 to 1860, Hadleigh was the home of James Murrell, thought to be the last and most famous male witch in Essex. Born the seventh son of a seventh son, he was known as Cunning Murrell and enjoyed a lucrative career as a white magician. He had great knowledge of plant remedies, which proved to be most effective. People from all over East Anglia would make their way to his cottage to be healed. He used his 'magic mirror' to find lost valuables and took great pride in his special telescope, which he boasted could see through walls. He had a copper charm which he believed could decide whether the person before him was honest.

Murrell often boasted that he was 'the Devil's Master', claiming that he had the power to exorcise spirits and overcome witchcraft with counter-spells. In his youth, Murrell had worked for a chemist in London, which was where he had acquired some knowledge of pharmacy and plant remedies. Murrell was known to be a secretive man with some odd habits. He never went anywhere without his old umbrella, whatever the weather.

No one was allowed near his piles of dusty old books, which were scattered around his cottage. Many were treatises on charms and spells and ancient medical volumes. He was well known for his iron witch bottles, into which he put samples of the urine, fingernail pairings, blood and hair of clients whom he had diagnosed as being bewitched. At midnight, the mixture would be heated to boiling point in absolute silence. This was intended to create a burning sensation in the witch's body, which would force her to remove the spell. One story relates how a girl was brought to him barking like a dog after being cursed by a gypsy girl. When Murrell heated up his witch bottle that night, it exploded and the next day the charred body of a woman was found lying in a nearby country lane.

Betty Puttick mentions Cunning Murrell in her book *Ghosts of Essex*:

> Murrell himself died on the day he prophesied, 16 December 1860. He was buried on the east side of the little Norman church in Hadleigh with his wife, who predeceased him in 1839 and some of his fourteen children, and his memory is still as green as the unmarked grassy mounts in that traffic-bound oasis.
>
> His reputation was so powerful, far beyond the isolated little village where he lived, that local people must have found it hard to believe that Cunning Murrell had gone at last. Indeed for years after his death they say a familiar small figure in an old blue frock coat and hard glazed black hat like sailors used to wear was sometimes seen as the light was fading, gathering herbs from the hedgerows and putting them in a frail basket hanging from the handle of a gingham umbrella.

Although the witchcraft laws were removed from the Statute Book in 1736, the fear of witches continued, particularly in remote country districts. The Victorian era was vastly different from that of the earlier witch-hunting years, yet fear and superstition were not very far away.

In 1863, in Sible Hedingham, which then consisted mainly of agricultural labourers, there lived an elderly deaf mute who was believed to be French. There were many rumours about his past – some said that his tongue had been cut out when he was a young man fighting for the French – but no one knew very much about him. He lived in a small mud hut on the outskirts of the village. Some referred to him as Dummy and he was a figure of curiosity, wearing very odd clothes and usually accompanied by a couple of dogs. As he was unable to speak, he communicated by signs, waving his arms about frantically. He seemed to scrape a living by fortune-telling.

On a warm August evening, the old man was enjoying a drink in the taproom of the Swan public house. Emma Smith, a young woman from the nearby village of Ridgewell who was married to a beerhouse keeper, was standing nearby. She suddenly started shouting at Dummy, complaining that she had been ill for many months and that her illness had been caused by the old man. She reckoned that he was a witch and had cast a spell on her. She begged him to remove the curse, even offering him gold sovereigns, but Dummy would not co-operate. The large drinking crowd loved the spectacle and were enjoying the fun.

At closing time, as Dummy was leaving the Swan, Emma Smith grabbed a stick and hit Dummy. She pushed the old man into the brook that ran alongside the pub. As he tried desperately to climb out from the opposite bank, Samuel Stammers, Emma Smith's friend, rushed to the other side of the brook to cut off his exit. Smith and Stammers once again took hold of Dummy and pushed him back into the water. The mood of the bystanders, who had been encouraging the pair and throwing stones, began to change as they realised what was going on. One shouted, 'If someone does not take the old man out, he will die in a moment.' Stammers, perhaps coming to his senses, jumped into the brook and pulled Dummy from the water.

Dummy was taken home but was found next day in an appalling state, badly bruised and shocked. The police were called and Superintendent Thomas Elsey had the old man taken to Halstead Workhouse, where he died of pneumonia on 4 September. Smith and Stammers were charged with having 'unlawfully assaulted an old Frenchman commonly called Dummy, thereby causing his death'.

On 8 March 1864, Smith and Stammers stood in the dock at the Essex Assize court in Chelmsford. Both were sentenced to six months' hard labour. The court questioned whether Dummy was a witch. Inspector Martyn Lockwood from the Essex Police Museum has thoroughly researched the case:

> Certainly he played on the superstitions of the local people. He was consulted by the local girls as a recognised authority on courtship and marriage; and when police searched his home they found numerous scraps of paper with various queries written on them. One such query read: 'Her husband left her many years and she wants to know whether he is dead or alive.' Even 130 years ago, in rural Essex the fear of witchcraft was a firmly held belief in the minds of country people.

Canewdon

Much has been written about George Pickingill (sometimes spelt Pickingale), who was referred to by locals as Old Picky. He was a farm labourer who lived in Canewdon, which a century ago was still believed to be at the heart of Essex sorcery. There was a local tradition that as long as the great tower of Canewdon church stood, there would be six witches in the village, 'three in silk and three in cotton', under the leadership of a Master of Witches, who must be a man. Writer Eric Maple described Pickingill as:

> the last and perhaps greatest of the Essex wizards. He was a tall and unkempt man with very long fingernails and intense eyes. He was solitary and uncommunicative and practised openly as a cunning man, restoring lost property and curing warts and other minor ailments by muttered charms and mysterious passes.

Maple also felt there was a darker side to the old wizard. He was believed to be descended from the witches of Canewdon, and it was said that hares ate from his hand and that he possessed the power of the evil eye. Villagers were allegedly in fear and awe of his magical powers. If he wanted water drawn from the village pump, the local boys would run to do it because they believed he could make people ill just by looking at them. Maple claims that Pickingill wandered around the fields threatening to bewitch the farm machinery. The farmers bribed him with beer to stay away. However, when he chose to work, it was said that Pickingill could cut a whole field of corn in half an hour, using his imps and familiars to do the job while he sat in the hedge smoking his pipe.

When, in 1909, the old wizard lay dying, he made a promise to all those gathered around his bedside that he would finally prove his extraordinary power. As the funeral hearse drew up at the churchyard, the horse walked away from the shafts and galloped off down the road, much to the amazement of the mourners gathered at the lych-gate.

George Pickingill outside his cottage in Canewdon.

THREE

CALENDAR CUSTOMS

To everything there is a season and a time... Ecclesiastes 3:1–8

Essex has an unusually fascinating folklore heritage. Many of the traditions we celebrate throughout the year are linked to religious festivals and ceremonies. Others are perhaps a little more irreverent, rooted in our pagan past and linked to the history of the county, which has survived the onslaught of Roman, Saxon, Viking and Norman conquests.

Whether sacred or secular, certain of our customs and superstitions that have been passed down through generations may appear to be rather strange signposts to our county's past. Some are ancient, others are relatively modern, initiated or revived for the tourist market. But it would be foolish to dismiss any of these traditions as irrelevant, for in time they will surely be absorbed into the annual cycle of our county folklore.

January

New Year

The passing of the old year and the birth of the new have great significance in Essex towns and villages, as in other parts of Britain. Celebrations for New Year's Eve often continue into New Year's Day without a break. In many parts of Essex, the chiming of church bells at midnight and the singing of 'Auld Lang Syne' are traditional ways of saying goodbye to the old year and welcoming the new – much the same as celebrations the world over.

Since the Millennium celebrations, it is now something of a tradition for some Essex folk to drive along the A12 to London to see in the New Year in

Trafalgar Square. At the stroke of midnight comes the hooting of horns, singing and New Year greetings. Over the last few years, too, molly dancers from Essex have congregated in Trafalgar Square to dance the New Year in as part of their special way of celebrating. Many revellers join in the jigs. Some may prefer to welcome the New Year quietly at midnight church services or stay at home to celebrate with family and friends. Fortunately, since 1974, New Year's Day has been a public holiday throughout the UK, giving people a chance to catch up on their sleep.

Although Essex is far distant from Scotland, many Scottish traditions are celebrated in the villages around Brentwood, Chelmsford and Colchester, particularly at New Year. This is a result of the influx of Scottish families to the area in the late Victorian period. They came to take over empty farms during the terrible agricultural depression which was caused by a combination of plummeting wheat prices, disastrous harvests and the importation of cheap corn from abroad. It left local farmers destitute and some sought work in the towns or in industry. More than 300 Scottish families settled into farms in Essex from the 1880s until the 1930s.

One Scottish tradition is first-footing. When New Year's Day arrives, the first-footer is welcomed to bring luck to a household. The custom calls for a tall, dark-haired man to cross the threshold immediately after the midnight chimes, bringing with him the symbolic gifts of a loaf of bread, a lump of coal and silver coins, to ensure that his hosts will have food, warmth and prosperity throughout the coming year. Entering in silence, he then wishes everyone present a Happy New Year, with a kiss for the ladies. Most importantly, he must leave by the back door. This is a Colchester version of a well-known first-footing rhyme:

> I wish you a happy New Year
> A pocketful of money, a cellar full of beer,
> A good fat pig to last all year
> So please give a gift for New Year.

Beginnings are important. Even non-superstitious folk regard the beginning of a New Year with a certain deference and 1 January is a key turning point in many people's lives. Essex newspapers are full of information advising on New Year's resolutions. This is now the day to start that new diet, a day for tidying up, a clean page in the diary on which, hopefully, splendid and happy things may yet be written. Divination rituals abounded in the old, more superstitious, days and even in this sophisticated world, good luck signs are sought.

In Essex newspapers and magazines, we now expect to see full horoscope predictions with upbeat speculation for the year ahead. Not since the Middle Ages has the 5,000-year-old craft of astrology been as popular as it is today. It derived its authority from complex mathematics and philosophical speculations appearing in the London and county almanacs and, until about 200 years ago, almost every king had at least one official astrologer, whose duty it was to study the heavens and keep his master informed of the future as foretold by the stars.

By the early twentieth century, astrology seemed to have almost disappeared from public view until it was revived by a press stunt at the time of the late Princess Margaret's birth in August 1930. The *Sunday Express* commissioned an astrologer, R.N. Naylor, to draw up a birth chart for the royal baby and to compile a simple horoscope for those born around the same time. The public response was enormous and horoscopes became big business as newspaper circulation figures soared and newspapers all over the world began publishing regular columns of astrological predictions.

People enjoy themselves as much as they can at the year's start, in the half-acknowledged but widely held belief that good luck at the beginning of the year ensures that good fortune will continue to its end. Every society seems to have its own rituals associated with New Year and it is a minefield of superstition in Essex, as in any other part of the country.

An old custom, collected from Colchester but doubtless not exclusive to the county, involves bowing to the new moon. Also, turning over silver coins in one's pocket will 'guarantee' that they will double their value by the end of the month. If with friends, the first person to glimpse the new moon should kiss one of his or her companions without delay. A gift can then be expected. However, absolutely no good will come of looking at the moon through the branches of a tree or through glass.

Other New Year superstitions depend on the notion that whatever happens at this magical time sets the pattern for the rest of the year. An old Colchester belief is that it is unwise to welcome in the New Year with no food or drink in the cupboards – for they will remain bare over the ensuing twelve months. The same applies to money. It was believed that the fire should not be allowed to go out during this first night of the year, lest the hearth remain cold permanently. Wearing new clothes at the start of the year was also believed to summon good luck. To break anything on this day – particularly a mirror – was considered to be a bad omen.

In many Chelmsford families – as indeed probably countywide – the cry of 'White Rabbits' upon waking on the first morning of each month was thought to bring luck, especially so on 1 January. Some annoy friends and family with 'A pinch and a punch on this first day of the month – and no return!' but this operates only until noon.

An interesting old January custom from Maldon was the presentation of a gift of wildfowl and oysters to the King's Vice-Admiral of Essex. This event is included in the autobiography of Sir John Branston in 1688, but whether it was an act of prudent diplomacy or an offering meant to ensure a bountiful harvest in the coming year is unknown.

The Mad Maldon Mud Race is a tradition that originated on New Year's Day in the early 1970s and has grown in popularity over the years. It started as a youthful dare made at the Queen's Head pub, which stands on the Hythe quay. The challenge to the young men was to serve a meal on the saltings of the river Blackwater while dressed in full evening dress. The challenge was accepted and carried out. The following year, from a bar on Maldon saltings, around twenty people made a 'mad dash' across the river bed, drank a pint of beer and then returned, and this was the beginning of the annual Maldon Mud Race, which

Maldon Mud Race, January 2005

Maldon Mud Race, January 2005

has turned into an annual sponsored event in which competitors can choose their own charity for half the money they raise. The other half is donated to local community charities picked by the Maldon Lions and Rotary Clubs. In 2005, more than 7,000 spectators, many from around the world, packed the promenade at Maldon to watch 180 competitors – dressed as waiters, clowns, nurses and a fully robed vicar – brave the 400-yard course, which was completed in around three minutes.

Epiphany

The last feast of the Twelve Days of Christmas is Epiphany, celebrated on 6 January. This is an important date on the Christian calendar, which commemorates the coming of the Magi. For the less religious, Epiphany is the traditional time to hoist the poor old Christmas tree out into the cold garden, throw away the tinsel, pack up the tangle of tree lights, remove the dusty cards and scrape the children's snowy stencils from the windows.

Plough Monday

'Speed the plough' is an old tradition that once took place regularly on the Monday after Twelfth Night, when farm workers began the working year and the winter ploughing started. A corn dolly, fashioned from the last stalks of the previous harvest, was laid in the first furrow and ploughed into the earth. This was done so that the corn goddess, whose spirit was believed to reside in the corn dolly, would look kindly on the farmers and ensure that the forthcoming harvest would be bountiful.

A plough was pulled around the village by local farm boys, with a view to collecting tips or 'largesse' from the farmers and gentry who employed them. It was wise to contribute even a few coins, as those who did not might find their front gardens ploughed up in retribution. Traditionally, the money would have been spent on beer in the village alehouse. In North Essex, the plough was usually painted white and kept in the local church. For this reason, the tradition became known as the White Plough.

The Molly Gang from Good Easter village are a familiar and popular group from the Rodings area, near Chelmsford. They revived the Plough Monday tradition in their area in 1980 and each year tour a different route, visiting local schools and, of course, a selection of pubs in the area. In Billericay, the custom has recently been revived by the Mayflower Morrismen, who, on the Saturday nearest Plough Monday, dance near the ancient Red Lion pub in the High Street, accompanied by an old plough borrowed from the famous Barleylands Farm Museum.

Calendar Customs

Right: A typical Essex corn dolly.

Below: Plough Monday – with a plough in the foreground.

Jeanette Peaty and Bob Dobney celebrate Burns Night in Essex.

Burns Night

Because of the large Scottish contingent in Essex, Burns Night festivities, celebrating the birthday of poet Robert Burns, are held in many towns and villages on 25 January.

February

Candlemas Day

This Christian festival was once regularly celebrated on 2 February. It commemorates the Purification (churching) of the Virgin Mary forty days after the birth of Jesus. Until the 1960s, mothers in many East London and Essex hospitals were asked if they would like to take part in the churching or Thanksgiving service in the hospital chapel as soon as they were able to do so, even if they were not regular churchgoers. Often they carried lighted candles on their way into the chapel.

The Essex agricultural and pastoral calendar still recognises Candlemas and at least one old gardener from Thorpe-le-Soken remembers the traditional rhyme:

> If Candlemas Day be fair and bright,
> Winter will have another flight.

> If Candlemas Day be clouds and rain,
> Winter be gone and will not come again.

At one time, the Christmas season did not officially end until Candlemas, and decorative evergreen branches were left in place until the eve of this festival, when superstition insisted that every trace of them be removed. Although not an Essex man, Robert Herrick's poetry reinforces some of our county traditions and reminds us of the fusion of pagan and Christmas customs, as in his poem 'Ceremony upon Candlemas Eve':

> Down with the rosemary, and so
> Down with the bays and mistletoe;
> Down with the holly, ivy, all
> Wherewith ye dress'd the Christmas hall;
> That so the superstitious find
> No one least branch there left behind;
> For look, how many leaves there be
> Neglected there, maids, trust to me,
> So many goblins you shall see.

St Valentine's Day

Beloved by greetings card manufacturers and florists, this festival, celebrated on 14 February, grows more popular by the year, receiving enormous attention from the media. Essex youth celebrates this day along with other romantics of the world. St Valentine's Day cards were introduced during the eighteenth century and are now sent in their millions, even more so since the advent of the Internet. Dances are traditionally held on St Valentine's Day and nowadays there are also the recently introduced – but much less romantic – speed-dating parties, where people are given the opportunity of meeting potential lovers in three-minute sessions, with a view to lasting love.

In centuries past, it was traditional in upper-class circles to give gifts on this day. There are interesting well-documented diary notes by Samuel Pepys – a regular visitor to Essex – complaining of the expense of being obliged to buy Valentine's Day gifts for lady friends, comprising expensive silk stockings and gloves.

When people lived in the county's smaller, more close-knit communities and the population was less mobile, the chances of already knowing one's future spouse were high. In Harlow, High Roding and Chelmsford, the following verse is known to have been sung on Valentine's Day:

> Good morrow, Valentine!
> God bless you ever.
> If you'll be true to me
> I'll be the like to thee,
> Old England for ever.

Shrovetide

The date of the Christian festival of Easter is fixed by the phases of the moon and can shift around by almost a month. The three days before the Lenten fast starts on Ash Wednesday were known as Shrove Sunday, Collop Monday – when fried 'collops' or slices of meat were eaten – and Shrove Tuesday, so named because it was the day on which Christians received absolution for confessing or 'shriving' their sins.

On Shrove Tuesday, after a church service, there was pre-Lenten jollity in feasting on the kind of food which was forbidden in Lent. This took the form of pancakes made from any perishable food left in the cupboard, which was forbidden in the forthcoming strict fast. Eva Baxter remembers that, when she was a little girl in Great Warley before the First World War, she was told that eating three pancakes on Shrove Tuesday would bring good luck for the coming twelve months.

In parts of North Essex, village sports and general merrymaking took place on Shrove Tuesday. Today, pancake races are held in some areas. In Billericay's new Archer Hall, Sheila Bailey, a member of the Emmanuel church, organises teams of pancake racers – of all ages – who toss pancakes in an attempt to win a prize and the Emmanuel Pancake Plaque.

This is an old rhyme from Great Dunmow:

> Shrovetide is nigh at hand
> And I be come a'shroving;
> Pray, dame, give something,
> An apple, or a dumpling.

Ash Wednesday was the start of forty days of austerity leading up to Easter. During this period, Sundays were not counted as part of Lent but as days of normality or even celebration. Today, as in the past, many people give something up for Lent.

Lenten charities and doles were common in the sixteenth century. At Clavering in 1537, John Thakes directed that barrels of white and red herrings should be given to the poor of the village to help feed them over the forty-day fast and a similar herring bequest was left by Lord Rich to Felsted and two adjoining parishes. Rich also founded Felsted School in 1564 and, two years later, set up a foundation to build almshouses.

March

St David's (Dewi) Day

A tradition associated with 1 March, St David's (Dewi) Day, is the wearing of one of the national symbols of Wales: a leek, worn in the hatband, or a daffodil, worn in the buttonhole. Just after the Second World War, there was an inflow of Welsh teaching staff, particularly to Ilford, Barking, Dagenham and surrounding schools, and former pupils remember their teachers sporting a daffodil marking their national day.

Mothering Sunday

This day occurs in the middle of Lent and is now universally celebrated. Originally, at a time when many young Essex girls were in service and boys had live-in farm jobs, people were given the day off to visit their families and attend their village church service. Even at the beginning of the last century, Mrs Minnie Heseltine, wife of the wealthy squire at Goldings in Great Warley, would make sure that her maids and farm workers took a simnel cake home to their families. There is an old Essex rhyme that mentions this traditional cake:

> I'll to thee a Simnel bring,
> 'Gainst thou go a-mothering,
> So that when she blesseth thee,
> Half that blessing thou'lt bring me.

Easter

It seems odd that Good Friday, which commemorates Christ's crucifixion and is the most mournful day in the Christian calendar, has become a cheerful public holiday in much of the UK. Jon Ellis, who spent much of his childhood in Brentwood, recalled that 'Years ago, most of the shops in the High Street were shut on Good Friday as a mark of respect, but these days nearly every shop is open for business'. The tradition of closing on Good Friday prevailed in many high streets around Essex until recent times. Many people still consider Good Friday to be the traditional start of the growing year and on allotments and vegetable patches all over the county, enthusiastic gardeners prepare their soil in readiness for sowing parsley and peas and planting potatoes.

Across Essex, as in many other places, hot cross buns are traditionally eaten on this day. It was once believed that any buns that were left over would remain fresh forever because they were marked with the holy cross:

> Hot cross buns! Hot cross buns!
> One a penny, two a penny, hot cross buns!
> Give them to your daughters, give them to your sons.
> One a penny, two a penny, hot cross buns!

An unusual tradition that goes back 100 years is known as 'hanging the hot cross bun' and takes place in the fifteenth-century Bell Inn in the heart of the lovely little village of Horndon-on-the-Hill. The custom started at the beginning of the last century, when Jack Turnell took over the pub. It was Good Friday and Jack marked the occasion by hanging a hot cross bun from a beam in the saloon bar. The tradition continued even during the Second World War, when a concrete bun bore witness to the shortage of food. Now, the large collection of hanging buns is part of the decor of this ancient inn. The practice continues every Good Friday, with the oldest person in the village – or at least the oldest available on the day – being ceremoniously hoisted up to 'hang the bun', to tremendous applause.

A century ago, communal skipping was a traditional Good Friday custom in the Saffron Walden area, as it is today on the promenade at Scarborough and other places in England, where everyone joins in to skip with huge ropes until dusk.

In towns and villages across Essex, morning church services are held on Good Friday, followed by church processions. Members of Churches Together in Billericay, carrying crosses and banners, customarily take part in the moving, Silent Walk of Witness, which winds its way through the High Street. At the lovely Emmanuel church, members remove the greenery from the huge Christmas tree that has been cut and formed into a cross. This bare cross is then decorated with white lilies prior to the Easter Sunday service of worship.

Easter has the most important religious significance in the Church calendar but in Essex this festival is celebrated in secular ways, such as egg rolling or pacing. 'Pace eggs' or 'peace eggs' derive from *Pasche*, the Latin-based medieval word for Easter. This tradition was once associated with folk in the north of England. In recent years, Easter egg hunts are organised around the county and are a regular occurrence in Colchester, Chelmsford, Clacton and Southend.

The predominant custom at Easter is the giving and receiving of chocolate eggs. These were not available to Essex families during the Second World War due to rationing (which did not end until February 1953) but in Dagenham, Mary Bray made sure her five young daughters enjoyed their Easter breakfast:

> During the war, when it was impossible to get hold of chocolate eggs for the children at Easter, we used to hard-boil hens' eggs, and add onion-skins to make them yellow, cochineal to make them red or pink. A popular custom also was to 'blow' eggs by inserting a needle through the top part of the shell and the bottom, blow the contents through a hole in the bottom and then the children decorated them.

Sheila Bailey with the cross decorated for Easter Sunday at Emmanuel church, Billericay.

Lady Day

Lady Day, 25 March, was an important date in the farming calendar until the twentieth century, as Essex was regarded very much as an agricultural county. Lady Day is the first of four traditional English quarter days in the year, the days when farm rents were paid and legal transactions took place. It takes its name from the Feast of the Annunciation. Before 1752, when the country moved from the Julian calendar to the Gregorian calendar, it was also the start of the year. A vestige of this remains in the United Kingdom's tax year, which starts on 6 April, i.e. Lady Day adjusted for the lost days of the calendar change.

April

April Fool's Day

This custom is celebrated universally and BBC Essex usually devotes part of its programme to April fool topics on this day. People in Essex enjoy practical jokes and hoaxing by the media has come to be expected at this time. If you fall for them, you are an April Fool – but only until midday. As the old rhyme goes, 'April Fool's Day's past and gone; you're the fool for making one!'

St George's Day

On 23 April, Essex, along with the rest of England, celebrates the feast day of St George, that enigmatic Christian soldier who was killed for his faith on 23 April 303 at Lydda, Palestine, so the legend tells us. St George was reputed to have rescued the daughter of the King of Silene when she was in danger of being a sacrificial victim offered to a dragon which was devouring the people. When St George arrived on his white horse, he beheaded the dragon with his sword and saved the princess. The legend of St George and the Dragon is believed to date back to the twelfth century but John Aubrey, writing in the 1680s, was doubtful about the authenticity of the story:

> To save a mayd, St George the Dragon slew,
> A pretty tale if all is told be true,
> Most say there are no dragons; and this say'd
> There was no George; Pray God there was a Mayd!

The stained-glass window at St Andrew's church at Wormingford shows St George rescuing a maiden from a crocodile. He is credited with performing miracles. On St George's Day, the Billericay Mayflower Morrismen celebrate by enacting a mumming play with all the traditional characters, such as St George, the Doctor and the Turkish Knight.

Since the new millennium, there have been repeated attempts to persuade English people to celebrate St George's Day by flying flags or wearing a rose, and frequent newspaper complaints about the lack of a national holiday. Local celebrations were fairly common in the 1930s but faded out again after the Second World War. The flag of St George – a red cross on a white ground – has been taken over by English football fans as a national symbol.

Increasingly, many Essex residents hoist the English flag and patriotic Essex people wear a rose in their buttonhole. Aubrey Temple from the Royal Society of St George's Wickford branch joins other Essex members in attending local church services, followed by a trip to London's Cenotaph, where a wreath is laid. Younger branch members join navy, army and Air Training Corps cadets in a march down Whitehall, followed by a service at Westminster Abbey.

May

May Day

The first day of May, formerly the Roman feast of Floralia and later the Celtic Beltane festival, is widely considered to be one of the most magical days of the year and was probably celebrated by the Romans in Essex.

There are many superstitious beliefs connected with the beginning of May. For example, it is thought that the crown of thorns placed on Christ's head during the crucifixion came from the hawthorn (*crataegus*) or May tree. May blossom was therefore never brought into the home, as it was felt to be unlucky. The sickly smell of the blossom is said to be similar to the smell that pervaded London during the Great Plague in 1665, from which many fled into neighbouring Essex.

Although May seems to have attracted this doleful history, there are in Essex more optimistic ceremonies. In Colchester, branches of May blossom were given to newly married couples to ensure protection against witches, while babies' cradles were often adorned with its early blossom. Certainly, it brings the Essex countryside alive with sweeping white flowers along our beautiful lanes.

With its origins in paganism, the May Day festival was temporarily abandoned in England in the mid-seventeenth century after the Puritans banned it and burned all the maypoles. However, the popularity of the event ensured its revival a few years later.

Enid Brown remembers a childhood verse sung on May Day at Basildon, between the two world wars, long before the huge housing estate was built:

May Day at Great Burstead in 1913.

> The First of May is Garland Day
> So please remember the garland
> We don't come here but once a year
> So please remember the garland.

Many older Essex folk remember the May Day festivities of their youth. Enid Brown remembers how some of the locals took a growing tree from the wood and brought it on to the village green to decorate with flowers and leaves. In modern times, dancing around the maypole has become a popular event once again at village fêtes, and at Ingrave crowning the May queen is a highlight of the afternoon.

Empire Day

Terry Parsons, who was brought up in Brentwood, remembered the importance of Empire Day, 24 May, when he was a lad in the 1920s. Empire Day was Queen Victoria's birthday and in later years was renamed Commonwealth Day. In Terry's time, the children, dressed in their best clothes, marched into the playground and saluted the Union Jack flag, which was ceremoniously hoisted on the school flagpole, and were given the rest of the day off.

Beating the Bounds

Beating the bounds at Rogationtide, a custom believed to date back to Saxon times, is enjoying a revival in many villages across the county. Covering the three days preceding Ascension Day, Rogationtide usually falls about forty days after Easter. In the days when people were illiterate and maps were rare among the ordinary folk, parish boundaries were usually marked by streams, trees, hedges or large stones and Rogationtide was the time for children to learn where the markers were – with the help of a little beating. Traditionally, parishioners set off to walk round the boundaries in large groups or 'gangs' led by the parish priest, who carried the cross. The walkers stripped wands of willow from the trees, garlanded them with milkwort – still known as gang or rogation flowers – and used them to beat the boundary markers. The children in the gang were lightly beaten too, and were also ducked in boundary ponds or streams – thus ensuring that their own patch was imprinted on their memories.

In Brentwood, when the parish was much smaller than today, 'beating the bounds' would not have taken very long. John Larkin, in his book *Fireside Talks about Brentwood*, tells how people would gather at the William Hunter memorial and proceed on a time-honoured route along the parish boundary line, which passed right through Mr Cottee's cottage. The procession entered his front door, marched through his home and went out through the back, the parishioners making their way down his garden path to the nearby brook, where the children were ducked. We have no idea what Mr Cottee's views were on the matter.

Oak Apple Day

Until the Second World War, Oak Apple Day on 29 May was remembered in parts of deepest Essex. The old tradition commemorates the day in 1651 when, following his defeat by Oliver Cromwell at the Battle of Worcester, King Charles II hid in a huge oak to escape his Parliamentarian pursuers. In honour of this event, loyal subjects took to wearing oak galls, or oak apples, on this day, to proclaim their Royalist sympathies after the restoration of the monarchy in 1660. Anyone failing to comply was beaten with swatches of stinging nettles. The custom has lapsed but Fred Eales, the well-known last harness-maker of Billericay, wore a sprig of oak leaves in his buttonhole to remind people of Oak Apple Day until his death in 1958.

Fred Eales, harness-maker of Billericay, 1895.

June

Weddings

Juno, the Roman goddess of marriage, gave her name to this favourite wedding month. There are many local traditions connected with weddings. A well known national superstition is that the bride must wear something old, something new, something borrowed and something blue. Something old ensures that the bride's friends will be faithful when they are needed, something new promises success in her new life, something borrowed means that she may take with her the love of her family, and something blue represents constancy.

Before the Reformation, the Church only allowed marriages to take place during thirty-two weeks of the year, skirting around the main church festivals. To marry at other times, couples had to obtain a special dispensation from the local priest.

The day chosen for a wedding was considered very important. Today, the most popular day in Essex is Saturday – convenience outweighs any lingering superstition – but one old Essex rhyme suggests:

> Monday for wealth
> Tuesday for health
> Wednesday the best day of all
> Thursday for losses
> Friday for crosses
> And Saturday no luck at all.

Since the 1994 Marriage Act, which allowed premises other than churches and registry offices to host marriage ceremonies, Essex has seen a huge increase in June weddings held in hotels, restaurants and many unusual venues.

The custom of throwing confetti is the modern version of showering the couple with rice and, as befits an agricultural county, wheat, corn and flowers at village weddings. Often the nave of the church was scattered with rose petals. Another tradition is that a kiss for the bride from a black-faced chimney sweep, universally regarded as a lucky figure, brings good luck. Mr Derek Williams, a popular Master Sweep from Pitsea, is happy to oblige.

One old county custom observed until the mid-Victorian era was 'blowing up the anvil'. When the village blacksmith married, neighbouring smiths fired a rejoicing salute by making a hole in their anvils, filling it with powder plugged well in – then exploding it. John Scrivener, the Bradfield blacksmith, made the usual preparations and recklessly forced the plug home with a hammer, which caused the powder to explode and the handle of the sledgehammer to be driven through his body, killing him instantly.

Pitsea chimney sweep Mr Derek Williams.

Wheat-whopping

We expect customs and traditions to be ancient but now and again a brand new custom hits the headlines, as it did in Blackmore at the time of the Queen's Silver Jubilee in 1977. A spot of 'invented' folklore to help local fundraising brought high jinks on the village green and attracted the national press and TV cameras to the village, when the 'ancient art of wheat-whopping' took place.

The rudiments of the 'sport' required the village maidens to parade on the village green in front of the band of wheat-whoppers. Each maiden was required to wear a garter which was inspected before the event. The maidens chose their station on the village green, consisting of bales of straw, buckets of water and bags of flour. At a given order, the whoppers sang the wheat-whopping anthem, during which handfuls of green wheat were ceremoniously dunked into a large tankard of ale. Then the chase was on. The wheat-whoppers chased the girls with the bunches of wheat and attempted to whop their hindquarters. Once whopped, the maiden had to surrender her garter to her pursuer. This continued until the hunting horn was sounded, a count of garters per whopper was made and the winner – and Chief Wheat-Whopper of Blackmore – was the person who had collected the most garters. As a result of the publicity, one group of women's libbers took offence. However, every now and again, this colourful custom comes out of mothballs and goes on to the Blackmore summer fête programme.

Wheat-whoppers on Blackmore Green, 1977.

July

Both the Fairlop Fair and the Dunmow Flitch Trials were held in July (*see* chapter one: Essex Traditions).

August

Lammas Day

> Behold, behold the summer has grown old,
> And with the harvest now begun,
> Lammastide – mix work with fun.

On many modern calendars, 1 August is still marked as Lammas Day. To town dwellers this means little, but to Essex farmers in past centuries Lammastide was one of the most active times of the year and signalled the start of the harvest season, the time when the first fruits or crops were gathered.

The word Lammas derives from 'Loaf Mass'. With the advent of Christianity in Britain, pagan rituals were officially replaced by church services or masses in which the first harvested grains were milled and baked into loaves of bread, taken to church, blessed and then offered as thanksgiving to God. The loaves were then shared among the congregation as a symbol of communal thanks for what would hopefully be a successful harvest. Lammas Day itself was a Christian holy day in Britain from Saxon until medieval times. A number of places in the county held fairs at this time and several parts of old Essex still have a Lammas Road, including Leyton.

There are some poignant old farming photographs of harvest time in Great Burstead and, thankfully, Essex churches celebrate this happy time of the year. Old beliefs and superstitions about county lore, taboos and rituals are deeply embodied in subconscious folk memory. The origins have often been forgotten but they still linger as part of the collective county memory.

Rural Essex folk believed the Harvest Spirit dwelt in the fields and that as the reapers cut the corn, the spirit was forced to retreat into the ever-dwindling remainder. No man wished to be the one who destroyed her refuge, so the reapers took turns to throw their sickles at the last stand of corn. It was then plaited into a woman's form – known as the Corn Dolly, Kern Baby, Ivy Queen or Harvest Queen, among other names. The figures were usually semi-human effigies, paraded around the field or placed on the wagon with the last load. The figure held the place of honour at harvest supper and was sometimes hung up in the farmhouse until the following year.

Harvest time – Dick Kent helping with the harvest (on horse), 1909.

September

Punch and Judy

Mr Punch is one folklore character that most children will immediately recognise. He and his long-suffering wife Judy, together with their baby, little dog Toby and a whole panoply of traditional characters, appear every September at Clacton, Walton-on-the-Naze, Frinton and other Essex coastal resorts.

Mr Punch goes back almost 400 years in this country and puppeteers were mentioned in Elizabethan times. In 1662, Samuel Pepys, a frequent visitor to Essex, described in his diary the appearance from Italy of Punchinello (soon renamed Mr Punch). This carved caricature of a hunchback with a shrill voice, who did dastardly deeds, has been popular among children ever since, but the 'politically correct brigade' has somewhat muted his activities.

Holidaymakers who visited Old Leigh Regatta during Septembers of the past will remember seeing Peter Pascoe, the Thurrock writer and puppeteer who entertained children as Professor Balbo at his regular site at Chalkwell. He carved his own cast of puppets, including Punch and Judy, and wrote the mini-dramas that so many children enjoyed. He carefully guards his method of making his 'swazzle', the metal device which, when held in the mouth, transforms the voice into Punch's screech.

Punch and Judy man, Professor Balbo, at Leigh Regatta.

Michaelmas

Michaelmas, which falls on 29 September in Essex although the date differs in other counties, is the grandly named Feast of St Michael the Archangel. In centuries past, tenant farmers in North Essex would be expected to give a goose to the farm owner. The Michaelmas goose is said to be at its prime at this time of year, fattened on a summer's lush grazing and the gleanings of the harvest field. A goose once formed part of the annual rent of a cottage or farm, traditionally payable at Michaelmas. The idea was perhaps to dissuade the landlord from raising the next year's rent. Michaelmas Day falls a week or so after the Harvest Moon, the full moon of the autumnal equinox. William Ward from Chelmsford remembers how, as a boy, he was told to stop picking blackberries at Michaelmas because 'otherwise left hanging, they will be spat on by the devil', a well-known Michaelmas saying.

October

Harvest Customs

Hone's *Everyday Book* for 1830 describes a contemporary harvest tradition that took place in several villages surrounding Chelmsford. At the conclusion of the harvest, a supper was provided, usually consisting of a roasted joint, plum puddings and copious supplies of good strong English ale. The proceedings opened with the singing of the following verse:

> Here's health to our master, the Lord of the feast,
> God bless his endeavours
> And send him increase;
> May prosper his crops, boys
> That we may reap another year,
> Here's your master's good health, boys,
> Come drink up your beer.

Several national folklore traditions cluster around this time of the year on the farming calendar. Although the harvest festival supper started in more rural districts of Essex, it is now a regular custom for many local town gardening societies to hold their harvest supper during October. In churches throughout the county, special harvest festival services are held and the churches are perhaps fuller than at other times of the year. Gifts of fruit, vegetables and flowers are brought to church to make simple decorations; there are bags of seeds, arrangements of autumn leaves – even old farm implements such as scythes and pitchforks are brought into church.

The Season of Hallowe'en

Hallowe'en, 31 October, is the Eve of All Hallows' or All Saints' Day. It was originally a season rather than a single night and was celebrated over the last couple of weeks in October. In the Essex farming fraternity, it was a time to prepare for winter. In medieval times, the local lord of the manor would gather his servants, tenants, soldiers and workers together to see who was under his control. At this time, he was expected to give a feast for everyone in his employ. Hallowe'en was an occasion when bonfires were lit to guide people home and welcome travellers to the hall. The Celtic name for this season was Samhain or Summer's End, a closing of the door to the year opened at Beltane or May Day and a gathering in of all crops.

In Essex there is now much 'tricking or treating', a relatively recent import from America, which is not popular with everyone. Many people in the village of Writtle will remember bobbing for apples by the eerie light of turnip lanterns. This Hallowe'en tradition still takes place occasionally at children's parties.

November

> No fruits, no flowers, no leaves, no birds, No-vember
>
> Thomas Hood

November is a time of mystic darkness. During Roman times, 11 November marked the beginning of winter. The Anglo-Saxon name for November was Blot-month, blood month, which probably derived from the custom of slaughtering cattle for winter consumption. In parts of Essex, horse fairs and markets were held during November, one being at the Halfway House Farm fields close to Brentwood.

Guy Fawkes

The novelist Daniel Defoe passed through Barking some time before 1722. He recorded his impressions of Eastbury Manor House in his book *A Tour Throughout the Whole Island of Great Britain*:

> A little beyond the town, on the road to Dagenham, stood a great house, ancient, and now almost fallen down, where tradition says the Gunpowder Treason Plot was at first contriv'd, and that all the first consultations about it were held there.

The Guy Fawkes link with Eastbury House, which is still a lovely mansion house at Dagenham, could have been Lord Monteagle. This staunch Catholic peer, who

Eastbury House.

is believed to have owned Eastbury House in 1605, received an anonymous letter thought to have been written by his brother-in-law Francis Tresham, one of the conspirators. It warned him not to attend Parliament on 5 November. A search of the vaults was made and Guy Fawkes – with his thirty-six barrels of gunpowder – was discovered. Fawkes was arrested for treason and tortured until he revealed his accomplices and the purpose of his insurrection, which was the introduction of a Catholic regime. He was executed on 31 January 1606, opposite the Palace of Westminster. The jubilant Government ordered thereafter that 5 November should be kept as a holiday, with special services, the pealing of bells and the firing of cannon.

Although these acts of remembrance were discontinued, the story of Guy Fawkes and the Gunpowder Plot are still celebrated nationally. Many Essex villages have communal gatherings at which bonfires are built. Collections are made to buy fireworks. Jack Bartlett remembers his childhood days in Thorpe-le-Soken just after the First World War, when, during most of October, the children built a huge pyre on the Brickfield and he and his brothers gained great pleasure from seeing their often creatively-dressed guy being burned on the enormous bonfire to the accompaniment of a fusillade from squibs and crackers:

> Remember, remember the fifth of November
> Gunpowder, treason and plot.
> I see no reason why gunpowder treason
> Should ever be forgot.
> Guy Fawkes, Guy Fawkes
> 'Twas his intent
> To blow up the King and the Parliament
> Three-score barrels of powder below
> Poor old England to overthrow

> By God's providence he was catched
> With a dark lantern and burning match.

Remembrance Sunday

Until 1945, this poignant tradition was known as Armistice Day and commemorated the anniversary of the armistice signed on 11 November 1918, ending the First World War. Since 1956, the day of commemoration has been the second Sunday of November. Many Essex war veterans and families travel to London's Whitehall to see the Remembrance Day ceremony at the Cenotaph. Flanders poppies, symbolising the bloodshed, are sold in aid of war invalids and their dependants. Many war memorials were erected in Essex in 1920 and people traditionally observe the two-minute silence, remembering those who died in the two world wars and in later conflicts.

December

On 1 December, the old Town Crier of Colchester used to announce:

> Cold December has set in,
> Poor people's backs are clothed thin,
> The trees are bare,
> The birds are mute;
> A pint of purl would very well suit.

The Cinque Port Liberty

The ancient maritime town of Brightlingsea is the only Cinque Port outside Kent and Sussex. It is a 'limb' of Sandwich, one of the original five ports. Each year a Deputy is chosen by the Freemen of Brightlingsea. He is the mayor of Sandwich's representative and, in the past, would have been responsible for maintaining law and order. The election takes place on Choosing Day, the first Monday in December, when the Freemen gather in All Saints church. At this ceremony, new inhabitants who have been resident for a year and a day can come forward to be 'recognised' and declared Freemen of the town. In July each year, the Deputy is confirmed into office, along with the Deputies of the other two limbs of Sandwich, in an historic ceremony in Sandwich's Guildhall.

Halcyon Days

In the old (Julian) calendar, 21 December was celebrated as the first day of the New Year. Even now, it holds significance as the shortest day of the year in the northern hemisphere, the time of the winter solstice, when the sun is at its furthest from the equator. Expecting wintry conditions, we are often surprised by how mild it is. This is what weather forecasters refer to halcyon weather. It is also St Thomas's Day and in Castle Hedingham on this day, old women went 'a-Thomasing' or collecting money.

Christmas

Advent is the beginning of the Church year for most churches in the western tradition. It begins on the fourth Sunday before Christmas Day, which is the Sunday nearest 30 November, and ends on Christmas Eve. It is a time of preparation in the religious lead-up to Christmas, before celebrating the birth of Christ. In the fifth century, it began on 11 November, St Martin's Day, and took the form of a six-week fast leading up to Christmas.

Historically, Advent was a period of quiet contemplation but this is rarely the case nowadays with visits to overcrowded shops and markets to buy presents, trees, decorations and other seasonal fare. In the twenty-first century, 'Christ's Mass' is obviously a time of celebration worldwide and in Essex, as in many other places, its religious significance has become buried under the trappings of an age far removed from that of centuries past.

The last Sunday before Advent is known as Stir Up Sunday, so called from the first two words of the collect, 'Stir up, O Lord, we beseech Thee, the hearts of Thy faithful people'. The timing coincided with the preparation of the Christmas puddings and cakes and Eva Baxter remembers the children in Great Warley singing on their way home from church:

> Stir up, we beseech thee,
> The pudding in the pot,
> And when we get home
> We'll eat it all hot.

Even in this day of convenience food, some Essex families keep to the old traditions and enjoy the ritual of making their own Christmas puddings. When Mrs Margaret Bray was ready to steam the Christmas puddings, each member of the family would ceremoniously stir the mixture three times in the direction of the sun's path – a biblical association with the Holy Trinity and the Three Wise Men. The inclusion of a silver joey, a threepenny bit, in the mixture was meant to bestow wealth on whoever bit upon it on Christmas Day.

With the county almost on the doorstep of East London, fashions and traditions which started in the capital reached Essex quickly. When you sit down to study your Christmas card list, you can either thank or blame that brilliant artist, inventor and Assistant Keeper at the Public Record Office – and perhaps the greatest entrepreneur that England has every known – Henry Cole, who made the Christmas card popular. In November 1843, this busy man realised that he was not going to have time to write the hundreds of personal letters that he usually sent to people every year at Christmas and commissioned the artist John Calcott Horsely RA to design him a card that could simply be signed and addressed. Horsley produced a lithograph 5½in long by 3½in wide that depicted the poor being clothed and fed, as well as a wealthy family drinking a Christmas toast. By December, 1,000 copies of the card had been hand-tinted and printed. Henry Cole took as many as he wanted and the remainder were put on sale in London at a shilling each. Within a few years, enterprising printers were producing printed Christmas cards, which were put on sale in Essex stationers and fancy shops, including the Great Eastern Stores owned by William Wilson in Brentwood and other Essex towns.

Before the traditional Christmas tree reached England, it was customary for county children to fashion a kissing bough. Hung from the ceiling on Christmas Eve, it took the form of a globe created from evergreen boughs fastened with twine. It was the seasonal centrepiece in many Essex homes, decorated with a ring of candles and a sprig of fresh mistletoe – another pagan custom.

The poet Frederic Vanson often wrote in *Essex Countryside* about the pre-Reformation custom of appointing a Lord of Misrule at Christmas. This character, chosen by the lord of the manor, acted as an unofficial motley fool, dressed in outrageous garments with a cap and bells, and chose his own 'court'. He played jokes on high-ranking people, with impunity, and could legally enter any house in the parish and there create disorder, without constraint. Henry VIII put a stop to this ancient custom, which was believed to descend from the Roman Saturnalia in celebration of the winter solstice that took place in parts of Essex.

Christmas Day itself is filled with all manner of customs, both local and national. The boar's head, cooked and elaborately dressed in its finery of greenery and garlands, was once the splendid centrepiece of feasts and banquets. Lynn Pewsey, in her book *A Taste of Essex* (1994) wrote:

> Up until 1868, in an ancient custom, the boar's head was the coveted prize in an annual wrestling competition held each Christmas Day at Hornchurch. It was cooked and prepared at Hornchurch Hall where the first slice was cut. Then in the afternoon, it was taken to the Mill Field perched on the prongs of a pitchfork and resplendent in a festive decoration of bay leaves, coloured ribbons and holly and with a fresh orange in its mouth, where the wrestling match took place.
>
> As many as 20 villagers are known to have taken part in the wrestling match and all were eager to win the head. The outright winner would be awarded the boar's

head which he then carried in triumph to his favourite hostelry where he and his friends feasted upon it with great merriment.

Easton Lodge was for many years the home of Lady Warwick, known as Darling Daisy, who was a friend of King Edward VII. She organised a Christmas party for her employees (50 house servants and 100 outside workers), together with their families and children from the village school. They gathered around a huge Christmas tree grown in Easton Lodge park. Lady Warwick enjoyed distributing presents, particularly to the children.

Boxing Day

Boxing Day on 26 December takes its name from the old and widespread tradition of giving a money tip, known as a Christmas box, to tradespeople or employees on this day. In 1846, Witham farmer Robert Bretnall gave £1 14s in Christmas boxes, which included gifts to his maidservant, the postman, singers, church bell-ringers and the church clerk and beadle.

In Clacton, for many years the Boxing Day Marathon took place on 26 December. This was organised initially by the Clacton Athletic Club. It is believed to have stemmed from the activities of a few Scouts in 1908, who decided to work off their Christmas excesses by going for a run on Boxing Day morning, covering a route from their meeting place in St Charles Hall, following the Holland Road out to Sea Lane and running back along the cliffs and coastline to their headquarters.

An ancient custom in which (usually) young village boys took part on Boxing Day or St Stephen's Day, 27 December, was known as 'hunting the wren'. It took place in various parts of Britain and was a cruel ritual which involved killing the bird, spiking it on a gorse branch and parading it around the village. In Essex, however, so the writer Humphrey Phelps tells us, the bird chosen was often a robin:

> The robin and the redbreast
> The robin and the wren
> If ye go tak' out of the nest,
> Ye'll never thrive again.

There are several versions of this piece of folklore. One origin of the custom is a Norse legend concerning a beautiful enchantress who bewitched men and lured them to their deaths in the sea. When an attempt was made to capture her, she took the form of a wren or robin and managed to escape, though not before a spell was cast upon her. As a result of the spell, she was compelled to reappear in the guise of a wren each St Stephen's Day, whereupon she would be killed by mortal hands.

FOUR

CURES AND REMEDIES

> Excellent herbs had our fathers of old
> Excellent herbs to ease their pain
> Alexanders and Marigold
> Eyebright, Orris and Elecampane.
>
> Rudyard Kipling

If the early herbalists are to be believed, the huge variety of plants that were grown in Essex could cure every ill – real or imaginary. There is hardly a substance known to man which has not at one time or another been taken as medicine, nor is there any disease for which folk-healers have failed to prescribe a cure. There seems always to have been a thriving interest in healing with plants; the herbalist's craft has a recorded history dating back more than 4,000 years.

Scholars tell us that when the Romans arrived on Essex's shores, they brought with them plants native to the Mediterranean, which must have previously been unknown to the indigenous Britons. Early herbal books outline numerous plants attributed to Roman gardeners, such as the rose, artemesia grapes, hops, clary (salvia) plus the herbs we use today, such as rosemary, bay, basil, thyme, dill and fennel. Contemporary Essex garden designer Stephen Hall used some of these plants in his prize-winning Roman garden at the Chelsea Flower Show in 2002.

Perhaps the Romans would have been interested in the plants growing naturally in our Essex clay soil. One plant that surely intrigued them is the one we know as woad (*Isatis tinctoria*) which, when the leaves were left to ferment, produced the blue dye that the Britons smeared over their bodies to frighten off the invaders. In 54 BC, Julius Caesar noted: 'All the Britons, without exception, dye themselves with vitrum (woad)'. Woad is a member of the mustard family and, as well as being a strong dye, woad's leaves were also included in ointments to soothe inflammation and ulcers.

Cures and Remedies

Steve Hall in his award-winning Roman garden at the Chelsea Flower Show.

Herbal medicine is a broad and fascinating topic of study, involving an accumulation of many different techniques, beliefs and superstitions, on which layers of cultural history have left a mark. A good knowledge of plant lore and herbs would have been necessary to cure a wide range of illnesses and diseases. Monasteries and abbeys, such as the first established abbey at Barking, founded in AD 666, were known to keep still rooms stocked with dried plants hung from rafters. Aromatic herbs were kept in pottles and other containers. Even small houses and farms had a special place, usually in the rafters, for keeping their dried plants in readiness for use.

As a cure for arthritis, Saxon physicians recommended an ointment made of goat's gall and honey. If that failed, they suggested incinerating a dog's skull and powdering the patient's skin with the ashes. For strokes, which they called the half-dead disease, they recommended inhaling the smoke of a burning pine tree. Many people still believe that the smell of burning pine cones improves their asthma.

The earliest information we have on the folklore of plants is found in the writings of herbalists and antiquaries. Black Notley, near Braintree, is proud of being the birthplace of the celebrated botanist John Ray (1627-1705), who, after studying at Cambridge University, produced not only the first book of flora covering the British Isles but also the *Historia Plantarum*, published in 1686.

A medieval herbalist.

Nicholas Culpeper (1616-1654), a contemporary of John Ray, was also educated at Cambridge and many of his plant cures were published in the *Complete Herbal and English Physician*, which has never gone out of publication. In the words of Dr Samuel Johnson:

> Culpeper, the man that first ranged the woods and climbed the mountains in search of medicinal and salutary herbs, has undoubtedly merited the gratitude of posterity.

A locally famous nineteenth-century Essex herbal doctor was Thomas Bedloe of Rawreth, who was known as the Dropsy Doctor and the Cancer Quack. A sign outside his cottage carried the advertisement: 'Thomas Bedloe, hog, dog and cattle doctor. Immediate relief and perfect cure for persons with the dropsy'.

'Essex has always been renowned for the great number and variety of its folk remedies,' wrote Alison Barnes in *Essex Countryside* magazine a decade ago. 'The most efficacious of these were the herbal cures, such as thyme tea for coughs, dandelion wine as a digestive and witch-hazel ointment for sprains, which can still safely be used today.' These cures were used by some Essex folk centuries after many of them appeared in the popular herbals of the time, and are probably still used today. Although many of the concoctions printed therein seem practical, many more are nonsensical, and others frankly unpleasant and even dangerous.

Above left: Essex pargetter Fred Willett finishing off a John Ray house panel.

Above right: John Ray's cottage at Black Notley.

In later times, Essex country folk became knowledgeable about plants for both culinary and medical needs. Of foremost importance was their power to treat and cure both injury and illness, for in isolated communities it was often costly and difficult to obtain medical help. There is little doubt that plants, trees and herbs would have been used as natural therapeutic aids. When medical knowledge was at a premium, folklore knowledge rose to the surface and individuals either treated themselves with family recipes, visited travelling bonesetters and herb women, or were helped by those in religious orders, who were sure to have herb gardens which provided the necessary substances for the treatment of ailments. Mary Gardiner, who was born in 1914, was brought up on a farm near Saffron Walden. She remembered:

> We rarely went to the doctor as he cost money. We learned how to use the plants growing in the countryside that had a host of other practical uses as well as being always there when money was short. We used dandelions, nasturtiums, sorrel and chickweed instead of vegetables. Seeds and flowers were used to make herbal teas and dandelion-roots and goosegrass could both be roasted to make a quite pleasant coffee. I seem to remember that the brambles could be used as a substitute for

string and I think they were used in broom and basket making. Nettles were used as vegetables and soup, and mother considered them a good spring tonic. Some people used them as flavouring for tea and beer, and I've even heard they were used in making army uniforms. Nettle leaves were also useful in dyeing material and wool.

County pamphlets and chapbooks are useful records of methods that were handed down through generations. Old wives' tales include the chewing of willow bark, the forerunner of aspirin; poultices and dressings made using mouldy bread, today's penicillin; boiled barley for water problems; and honey for open wounds. The medical journal *The Lancet* has, in recent times, published papers on studies using honey for the treatment of ulcers. St John's Wort (*Hypericum*) is also being studied as a treatment to combat depression. And that wriggly little black friend, the leech, is again being used in the treatment of blood disorders.

Dr Cornelius Butler (1789-1871), who kept a surgery at Cockayne House in Brentwood High Street for many years, as well as attending the paupers six miles away at the Billericay Workhouse, was a much respected larger-than-life character. On his huge white horse, he would make his visits to patients in the neighbouring villages. It is believed that he made his own medications and ointments and used leeches to treat his patients when he felt they needed relief in this way. He was once heard to say, 'I never believe in bleeding a man more than three times a day.' Modern research has shown that the leech – a mainstay of medicine from ancient times to the nineteenth century in the treatment of almost every disease, from whooping cough to madness – has an important role to play in plastic surgery. These bloodsucking worms are capable of absorbing three to four times their

Dr Cornelius Butler on his rounds.

own weight in blood. They also produce a natural anticoagulant that stops blood clotting. When plastic surgeons transfer or graft new skin onto a damaged area, the tissues usually become severely bruised and congested with blood. Applying leeches to reduce the swelling is considered by many doctors to be the safest way of dealing with the problem.

In the Cater Museum in Billericay High Street, there is a complete set of eighteenth-century medical instruments, which were highly regarded by the physicians of times past, displayed in an apothecary's cupboard.

Mary Clarke, who was born in 1910, remembered her grandmother using some strange ingredients from her 'household book', such as hedgehog fat, which was believed to be a good remedy for earache. A drop or two of the hot melted fat was poured into the affected ear at bedtime. It was held that certain types of deafness could also be cured in this way, as the fat would dissolve the hard wax and relieve the eardrum. If hedgehog fat was unobtainable, goose fat was sometimes used in its place and was said to be almost as good. Wild garlic was used as a cure for the first signs of a cold and it was invaluable for whooping cough.

Strange as it sounds, mice were included in some old 'receipt books' as remedies to cure whooping cough. There is an account from Colchester describing how mice were skinned, chopped up and fried and, in another case, baked 'in their

An apothecary's cupboard at the Cater Museum.

jackets' and given to sick children to swallow whole. One school of thought maintained that the young patients should be told what they were being forced to eat; another that the utmost secrecy should be observed and the cooked mice cunningly disguised in the food.

East Anglian writer Eliza Vaughan discovered, while researching herbal cures in Essex, that two young brothers suffering from ague (shivering fits) were cured by taking 'four fat spiders in a glass of gin, three times daily for a fortnight'. Their young sister had the unenviable task of collecting the spiders. A cure for whooping cough was to tie a caterpillar in a bag round the neck of the afflicted person. As the creature wasted away, so the sickness also disappeared. A variant of the spider cure was used by Elias Ashmole in 1681 when he became ill. He wrote on 11 April that year that he 'took early in the morning a good dose of Elixir and hung three spiders about my neck, and they drove my ague away'.

Cures to rid the body of warts and calluses come by the dozen and make fascinating reading. A Witham farmer's wife suggested that burying a piece of red meat in the garden and walking over it every day will make the warts disappear. Another remedy from Braintree during the eighteenth century stated: 'Do take and steal a bean pod without being seen and rub it on your warts. Then take and bury that where no man walketh. Do not let anyone see you a-doing of it and tell no one.' By this means, one Essex woman claimed to have been rid of twenty-two warts. Bathing warts with tincture of thuja or hops has been known to make them disappear. Fred Eales, the last harness-maker, who lived in Billericay High Street until he died in 1958, was the last of Lord Petre's ale-conners (inspector of ales). He was proud of his country origins and plant knowledge and, even when he was in his late eighties, could reel off many country recipes to cure rheumatism and warts.

Culpeper's wart cures were well known in seventeenth-century Essex. He advocated 'rubbing a black snail over the warts, nine times one way and nine times the other, then stick the snail on a blackthorn tree'. Paul Stevens, a contemporary Essex Romany gypsy remembers his mother using a very similar remedy to rid him of his childhood warts – and it worked.

Snail water was a well-known Essex remedy for consumption (tuberculosis). Hannah Woolley, who lived in Newport during the seventeenth century, gives a recipe for it in her book *The Queen-like Closet*, published in 1670. This involved grilling a peck of snails 'with the houses on their backs', crushing them in a mortar and then boiling them up in a mixture of ale and white wine, along with various herbs, a pint of earthworms, four ounces of hartshorn and ivory to make a porridge. By the late nineteenth century, snail water was usually known as snail gruel or broth and was made by simply boiling a few snails and a little barley in milk and adding honey to taste.

Honey Cure

Honey was plentiful in Essex and was an important ingredient in many country remedies because of its curative properties. There were more beehives listed in the Domesday Book in Essex than in any other eastern county. Honey is steeped in superstition and country lore, and rural folk depended on it for food and cures.

The old custom of 'telling the bees' was well known in Essex until the twentieth century and may still be observed in parts of the county. Kathleen Curtis from Colchester remembered:

> We knew we had to tell the bees whenever something important happened in the family. You were supposed to tap the hives and whisper to the bees, very gently, letting them know of the news such as a wedding, birth of a new baby or most sadly a death in the family, when a black ribbon was hung over the hive.

John Whittier's verse provides an atmospheric peep at the bee world of long ago:

> Just the same as a month before
> The house and the trees,
> The barn's brown gable, the vine by the door,
> Nothing changed but the hives of bees.
> Before them, under the garden wall,
> Forward and back,
> Went drearily singing the chore-girl small,
> Draping each hive with a shred of black.
> Trembling, I listened: The summer sun
> Had the chill of snow;
> For I knew she was telling the bees of one
> Gone on the journey we all must go!

The late Brother Adam of Buckfast Abbey, one of the world's most famous beekeepers and a friend to Essex mead-makers, once commented: 'Bees are the most mysterious creatures; they have a tendency to take offence if you don't include them as part of the family, in which case they will stop providing honey and may even desert you.' Bee stings were believed to ease the pain of arthritis and rheumatism.

Today, snakes still bask in the sun on the sea walls at Leigh when they eventually emerge from hibernation. They also live in the ditches and thickets of Essex, as in Moore's Ditch in the woodland behind the Viper pub at Mill Green, near Ingatestone. A television programme recently dubbed Essex 'the county of adders'. Information dating back at least two centuries indicates many beliefs about adders. They were said to be deaf, on the authority of Psalm 58: 'They are like the deaf adder that stoppeth her ear, which will not hearken to the voice of the charmer'. It is believed that if you kill an adder, its mate will seek you out, and that female adders swallow their young when danger lurks, then vomit them up once the danger is past. An adder coming to the door of a house is a death omen. Adder's oil was prized as a remedy for earache.

There is an unusual cure for the sting of an adder in the *Commonplace Book* written by Dr Benjamin Allen, a friend of botanist John Ray: 'the head of the same that bitt, bruised and laid to the place' or 'the flesh of the adder, given inwardly'. Dr Allen goes on to tell of his experience with a boy who was bitten by a mad dog. He was certain that the boy could have been saved by eating the mad dog's liver, fried.

Ralph Williams, in 1652, suggested a cure for yellow jaundice: 'Take elecampane roots, and the inner bark of the Barbery, of each six ounces; of Salendine root eight ounces; of English saffron the weight of a groat; seethe all these in a pint of white wine, strain it, and drink thereof four spoonfuls morning and evening.'

Talismans and amulets played an important part in folk medicine. Until the mechanisation of agriculture, labourers using the scythe often carried bloodstone, which they used for the treatment of cuts. It was also carried as an amulet against nosebleeds. Natural bloodstones are said to fall from the sky during nights when the Perry Dancers, or Northern Lights, can be seen. They are held to be the petrified congealed blood of the supernatural warriors whose combat appears as lights in the sky. The more usual bloodstone is a holed bead of glass or crystal worn as an amulet around the neck on a red silk thread that has knots tied in it at intervals of three inches. When someone is cut, the bloodstone should be rubbed against the wound to stop the bleeding. The bloodstone is an ancient Germanic tradition, which goes back at least 1,700 years. Bloodstones can be seen attached to the scabbards of Anglo-Saxon, Alemannic and other Germanic swords preserved in our museums. A similar tradition may account for the magic scabbard of King Arthur, who could not die of wounds as long as he wore it.

A remedy from Feering for a cut finger involved pepper sprinkled on the bandage. For a deep cut, it was customary to apply a slice of horseradish to it to arrest the bleeding, put pepper on the wound and then draw the edges of the cut back together to effect healing.

Fingernails and toenails often occur in ancient cure recipes. It was not always the rural folk who knew the secrets of curative properties. Samuel Pepys was a great believer in the old cures. He records in his diary a visit to Brentwood to see his old friend Cesare Morelli, who, as a practising Catholic at that sensitively religious time of 1680, was forced to leave London for safety reasons. Pepys had employed Morelli in 1675 as house musician and enjoyed his company very much. He made the tiring journey from London along the Essex Great Road, accompanied by Mr and Mrs Houblon, who also wanted to meet Morelli to commission him to compose songs and psalms for their young daughter Sarah to

Cures and Remedies

Above left: Romany gypsy Paul Stevens.

Above right: Brother Adam, champion bee-keeper and mead-maker.

Right: A bee skep.

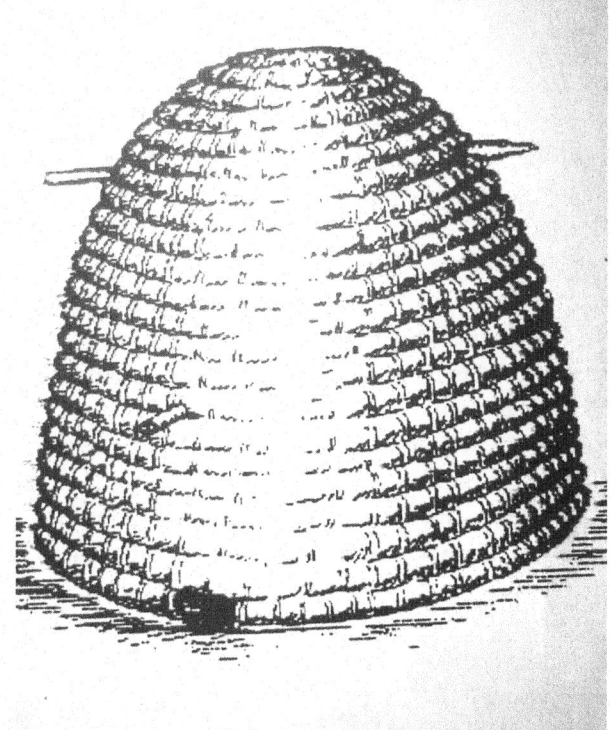

sing. As Morelli had been suffering from gout, Pepys had earlier visited a London healer 'possessed of miraculous sympathetic powers' and had been instructed to save parings of Morelli's toenails and three locks of hair to take back with him to London so that the healer could produce a cure. Pepys is also recorded as returning to Brentwood again with the cure, but this time accompanied by the infamous Lady Mordaunt.

White witchcraft spells and stone witch bottles containing nails and hair have been found, usually in the roof space or the walls or cemented over the door frames of cottages. One theory was that the witch had created a magical link with her victim using human body products such as urine, blood and nail parings.

As fingernails were important ingredients in some remedies, there were several local anecdotes and rhymes regarding them. The idea that it matters when you cut your nails is believed to date back to the sixteenth century. Most agree that Monday is the best day and Friday should be avoided. Kathleen Curtis in Colchester remembered this rhyme:

> Cut them on a Monday, you cut them for health,
> Cut them on a Tuesday you cut them for wealth,
> Cut them on a Wednesday you cut them for news,
> Cut them on Thursday a new pair of shoes,
> Cut them on Friday you cut them for sorrow,
> Cut them on Saturday see your true-love tomorrow,
> Cut them on Sunday the devil will be with you all the week.

Using urine to cure chilblains is probably world famous and is often recited by Essex folklorists and Romany gypsies. Even today, urine is used as a cure for many illnesses and was once baked in a cake or made into a paste with garlic to restore hair.

The Romany gypsies in Essex had a cure for a hernia, which involved passing the patient (usually a child) through an ash sapling, split through the middle, preferably one which had grown naturally from seed and had not previously been damaged by man. The tree was then tightly bound up and, as it grew together, so the patient would be healed.

In 1722, writer and journalist Daniel Defoe was on one of his rides through the Essex marshes, exploring the North Essex villages for his book *A Tour Through the Eastern Counties*. He gives an interesting account of one of the most prevalent ailments of the time, which he called 'dreaded ague'. The antidotes were strange: some folk were desperate enough to swallow live insects; others chewed gunpowder.

An old-fashioned cure for shingles, collected from an elderly lady in Paglesham who remembered her grandparents using it, was the 'abracadabra ritual'. It was employed in the marshland villages. The patient simply wrote down the word 'abracadabra' in large capitals and wore the charm around the neck on a silken thread for eleven days. It was then removed and flung into a fast-flowing river or stream. As the water bore the amulet away, so too, it was believed, did it carry off the illness. Such was the power of positive thinking.

More modern remedies included drinking cabbage water and nettle tea to purify the blood and liquorice powder to purge the system. Eva Baxter, who was born in 1908, remembers how, when she was a child, grown-ups seemed to be obsessed with bowels. She recalled that:

> It was believed that constipation was thought to be at the root of most illness and should be avoided. Every family had their own method. Ours was a Friday night dose of senna pods, placed in a glass and covered with water, left overnight, strained and drunk upon waking on Saturday morning. When this did not work, we would be given syrup of figs or castor oil.

She also remembers eucalyptus being sprinkled on her handkerchiefs and pillows at night when she had a bad cold:

> How I hated that eucalyptus smell! I remember I had to sip hot lemon with no sugar and it was awful. If I hadn't improved, the next day was spent in bed and then came the poultice which was made of warm mustard spread on brown paper and this covered my chest and back. It was very messy and the paper crackled and scratched every time I turned over in bed. Next came rings of raw Spanish onion – I dreaded getting a cold when I was young.

Hermit Cures

In centuries past, Essex seems to have attracted an unusual number of 'men of the road'. Dido was such a person; he roamed around the Essex lanes and fields from around 1880. He lived in Hainault Forest and was well known in the markets and pubs, where he peddled his wares in the small towns surrounding Epping. Using roots, leaves and flowers which he collected from the forest, he brewed up an assortment of potions in a large pot or cauldron hanging over an open fire. The resulting elixir was a much sought-after remedy which apparently cured all manner of ailments, from whooping cough to arthritic pains. Perhaps the most famed of his remedies was his green fern ointment. This was believed by local people to possess powerful healing and antiseptic properties and was applied indiscriminately to cuts, bruises, sprained ankles and sore eyes. It gave instant relief to burns and was supposed to cure chilblains overnight. Dido had once promised to pass on the recipe for making this unguent to a friend before he died, but in fact he never did and the secret was lost.

Dido the herbalist in Epping Forest.

Old Oddy lived in the woods near Childerditch, not far from Warley Barracks, during the 1920s. Wally Hull remembers seeing him in the woods when he was a child:

> He lived in an old hut made of branches and sacking. Without heat or electricity, he survived and was always cheerful. He loved a chat. He cooked all his food on an open fire and also knew how to use wild herbs and would sell bunches of watercress, which grew in the stream near his shack. He snared rabbits, selling them for sixpence in the Horse and Groom and the Thatchers, together with bunches of wild flowers and mushrooms. He reckoned the watercress growing near his home had special healing powers.

Later it was found that the stream passed through Warley Barracks and had a fair amount of sewage content.

Healing Waters

In earlier times, when people were sick or infirm, it was human nature to seek cures from any source, however unlikely. At a time when medicine was less the science that it is today, the creative powers of the natural waters found in some areas acquired a certain reputation. It was well known that people would travel long distances to visit spas and watering places such as Tunbridge Wells, Bath and Cheltenham, as well as watering holes on the Continent.

During the eighteenth and nineteenth centuries, Essex received unexpected attention for its natural water springs, which were believed to be imbued with medicinal, almost magical, properties. William Fitzstephen, in his book *History of London* (1180) wrote: 'Round the city ... arise excellent springs at a small distance, whose waters are sweet, salubrious and clear, and whose runnels murmur o'er the shining stones'.

Although Essex was not generally renowned for its waters, there was enough evidence and interest for the writer and historian Miller Christy to study the subject seriously. During the early years of the last century, he went on an odyssey around the county, seeking out natural springs. His findings are included in his book *Mineral Waters and Medicinal Springs of Essex* (1906). Christy located at least two dozen springs, although there were probably more, and carefully collected samples of water from each, taking them back for laboratory analysis. The results of the majority were disappointing. Among the many places visited were the springs at Gidea Hall in Romford and at Chadwell, whose name is derived from St Chad, patron saint of medicinal springs and wells. Christy spent time at Weald Hall, where the water was claimed to have a drying and astringent quality and was recommended for haemorrhages. The spring at Tilbury Hall was close to the side of a hill overlooking the River Thames and its waters were said to contain calcareous earth, true nitre, sea salt and mineral alkali, useful for treating gout and diseases arising from acidity. The Forest spring on the north side of

Weald Hall, 1900.

Above: The Upminster Common well.

Left: Hockley Spa.

Hainault Forest, in the parish of Stapleford Abbots, was said to contain purging salts, iron and sea salts, useful for 'bilious and nephritic colic', as well as for sore eyes and legs.

At Upminster Common, today signposted Tylers Common, there was a popular spring known to have existed from at least 1670, just 200 yards below the eastern boundary of Tylers Hall Farm. Famed as a medicinal spring, it was numbered among the three most efficacious in Essex and many people made their way there hoping to be cured of all manner of illnesses, from consumption to the pox. This mineral well was guarded by iron railings.

Hockley was another place that received special attention. Robert Clay and his asthmatic wife Letitia moved to the area in 1838 and Letitia's health improved so miraculously and so quickly that the owner of the land, a London solicitor named Fawcett, had the water analysed. He also discovered that an earlier cottage on the site had been inhabited by William Hazard, who had lived to age of 105, dying in 1808. On the strength of this, an attempt was made to establish a commercial spa at the site, which the owner hoped would rival the famous Bath and Cheltenham spas. During the 1840s, pump rooms were erected, advertisements were printed and a female attendant was installed, but the venture was unsuccessful and disappeared after a few years, although the pump room at Hockley still stands.

There was also a spring at Vange. Lynn Pewsey, in her book *A Taste of Essex*, writes:

> About 1900 'Vange Water' became a fashionable fad. Five wells were sunk on the site of a spring in Vange and the product bottled and sold at 2/3d a pint with extravagant claims for its health-giving properties. Edwin Cash the entrepreneur behind the scheme grew wealthy on the profits as a trusting public poured into Vange to sample this new cure-all, and orders for the bottles came from all over the world. The bubble soon burst, however, and Vange Water is now only a footnote in the history books.

Some startling tales of cures were told during the heyday of the Vange water scheme. One man is said to have drunk just a glass and then thrown away his crutches and walked.

Perhaps today's interest in old remedies is due to the often disturbing side effects of some of our modern prescribed medications. Over the last century, there has been a noticeable interest in homeopathy and a drift back towards reliance upon herbal remedies and the beneficial aspects of the living world.

FIVE

FOOD LORE

Famous for good land, good malt and dirty roads.

This was Daniel Defoe's description of Essex in 1722. John Norden, writing earlier, waxed lyrical about the county: 'This shire is more fatt, frutefull and full of profitable things, exceeding (as farr as I can finde) anie other shire, for the general commedities and the plenty.' That description explains why Essex had so many windmills, for where the corn grows high there must be stones to grind it.

Feasting and folklore go hand in hand and Essex is a county renowned for its interesting gastronomic and brewing history. Many of our age-old customs, culinary traditions and festivals have close associations with food, such as Colchester's annual Oyster Feast, the Dunmow Flitch Trials, the Hornchurch boar's head and Daniel Day's annual picnic at the Fairlop Fair, among others.

When the Romans invaded Britain and settled in Colchester, they must surely have been delighted to find such a huge diversity of food. Fish and oysters were there for the taking from our coastline and the numerous rivers and streams, and the woodlands were home to wild boar and birds. Having established their capital at Colchester, the Romans expanded local oyster production. Oysters were considered a great delicacy and the Romans enjoyed them and had enough to be able to export them to Rome, where they fetched a high price.

Cheese

The Romans were cheese-makers and it is likely that they brought the skill with them. During the seventeenth century, Essex farmers made cheese from cow's milk, storing it in special cheese lofts. At Ingatestone Hall, there existed the great West Cheese Chamber, which was lined with boards 'to keepe owt rattes'. At one time, farmers sold their surplus cheese in the London markets, where the street cry advertised it as coming 'from the meadows and marshes of Essex'. But Essex cheese-making declined during the agricultural revolution in the following century.

The Essex coastal marshes provided grazing for sheep, which were reared mainly for their wool but also valued for their milk which, when transformed into a hard cheese, kept well through the winter months. During the seventeenth century, the cheese was loaded on to wagons and sold over the London border in the markets. The ewes were milked in small huts on the marshes, known as wicks, and the word has become a part of several place names on the Essex coastline. With a welcome revival in cheese-making in recent years, Essex now produces some excellent farmhouse cheeses, including curd and goat's milk varieties from Rozbert Dairy at Pebmarsh on the Essex/Suffolk border.

Our county cheese was obviously not enjoyed by the poet and satirist John Skelton, who wrote:

> A cantle of Essex cheese
> Was well a foot thick
> Full of maggots quick.
> It was huge and great
> And mighty strong meat
> For the devil to eat.
> It was tart and punicate.

Sea Harvest

The fishing industry at Barking is mentioned in the Domesday Book. During the eighteenth century, the town was considered to be one of England's greatest fishing ports. In 1722, Daniel Defoe described Barking as 'a busy little port, fishing for the London market'. Its success until the mid-1800s was due, in no small way, to Samuel Hewett, that doughty son of Scrymgeour Hewett who had come from Scotland to Barking in 1760. When Samuel took over the family business at Barking, he ingeniously kept the fish on ice, sending the catch back to port in a fast boat while the trawlers stayed on their fishing stations. The ice was obtained by flooding the marshes above the town before the first hard frost, then breaking up the ice and storing it in icehouses. However, when the railway came to Essex, fish from other ports could be delivered to London faster than Hewett could transport it by road or river from Barking. The fishing port closed in 1899.

Harwich, Leigh and other small ports supply herring and flat fish, which end up in the many fish and chip shops around the county. People living on the Essex coast at the beginning of the twentieth century enjoyed fish at certain times of

A Barking fisherman.

the year, and no Sunday tea was complete without cockles and winkles served with brown bread and butter. Many people bought them directly from the cockle sheds at Leigh-on-Sea, near Southend.

The Whitebait Festival

Whitebait, which is the mixed fry of small fish of all varieties, but usually herrings, has for centuries been an esteemed delicacy from Essex. The first Whitebait Festival originated in Essex as a private annual dinner and was enjoyed by some of the gentry who had been connected with the costly schemes to repair the ravages of the great Thames flood of 1707, known as the Dagenham Breach. The host, Sir Robert Preston, the MP for Dover, invited distinguished guests to his fishing cottage nearby. The Prime Minister, William Pitt the Younger, became a regular visitor, but asked for a venue closer to London. To suit him, Greenwich was chosen and the local delicacy, whitebait, was adopted as an important part of the menu. Its annual day of glory was the Whitebait Feast, held until 1884 at Greenwich or Blackwell. Traditionally attended by leading politicians, the occasion marked the close of the parliamentary session and was held on Whit Monday or the nearest convenient day.

The Whitebait Festival was revived in 1934 by the Southend Chamber of Commerce, Trade and Industry. In the early days, the opening and the 'blessing of the catch' was held at the end of Southend Pier, but sadly this was destroyed in 1976. In modern times, this unique service, in which church ministers of five denominations take part, is held outside the Cliffs Pavilion in Southend, followed by the prestigious Whitebait Festival.

Herbs and Vegetables

Essex folk have long considered parsley to be a plant of evil omen and many superstitions have grown up around it, among them a belief that it is unlucky either to plant or transplant parsley.

The allium family, which includes onion, garlic, leek and ramson, is one of the most useful groups of plants, offering not only the healthiest of vegetables, but a cure for many illnesses. According to a seventeenth-century proverb:

> Eat Leekes in March and ramsons in May
> And all the year after physicians may play.
> (Aubrey, 1847)

This held true for Mrs Elizabeth Halley of East Ham, who rarely had a cold due to eating many forms of onion. Bulbs of ramsons (similar to garlic) were dug up when they first sprouted in spring, washed and dried, then packed into a wide-mouthed jar with dark brown sugar poured over them. The whole was stored in a pantry until the winter, when colds and influenza made life difficult.

Saffron is perhaps the most famous of culinary Essex plants. In times past, the fields of Saffron Walden were awash with the purple hue of the saffron crocus in flower. The flowers were harvested in October, before the petals were completely opened. The orange stigmas, the only part of the flower used, were separated and dried on racks over slow fires – 20-30,000 flowers would produce about 1lb of saffron. The flowers would be crushed and pounded into cakes. The purple petals covered the ground like massive blankets but the villagers knew that cultivation of the saffron would provide wealth and security for their families.

There is an interesting tale about how the first saffron corm was smuggled out of the Middle East by a pilgrim during the fourteenth century. He cleverly hid it in the hollow section of his staff. The lush arable land of Essex, known for the cultivation of barley and corn, was now host to a new and more lucrative market, a tenth of which would be given to the clergy of Walden, who made sure there was a tax on all saffron grown outside the abbey boundaries. Although no longer grown in the town, the saffron crocus is depicted on the walls of the Sun Inn as a testament to the lucrative influence of the flower in the history of the town.

Samphire is a delicious wild plant, with an ancient and fascinating history, steeped in folklore. Gathering the rock variety from cliffs was often a full-time, hazardous

A saffron crocus.

Saffron Walden pargetting.

occupation for many families during medieval times. Intrepid samphire-gatherers often fell to their deaths, a fact mentioned by Shakespeare in *King Lear*:

> Half way down hangs one who gathers samphire – a dreadful trade.

But in Essex, samphire is harvested safely from the salt marshes along many places on the Essex coastline, particularly around Maldon and Goldhanger, in early summer.

Around 1370, the Countess of Hainault sent her daughter, Queen Philippa,

Samphire.

wife of Edward III, a manuscript which set forth the virtues of rosemary:

> The leves leyde under the heade whanne a man slepes, it doth away evell spirites and suffereth not to dreme fowle dremes ne to be afeade.

Game

In Tudor times, when forest land covered much of the county, Essex was a favourite hunting ground for many English monarchs, from William the Conqueror to Queen Anne. In *A Taste of Essex*, Lynn Pewsey wrote:

> The ancient forests of Essex provided large quantities of game for the royal hunt, and until a couple of centuries ago, every monarch followed the chase in Essex. Though the penalties for poaching were severe, venison could be caught legally at certain times of the year; citizens of London were permitted to hunt in Epping Forest on one day a year, and from the time of Henry III, an extra day at Easter was allowed. The aristocracy had no such restriction, and by the end of the 16th century there were a hundred deer parks in Essex and Kent alone.

After the hunt, the choicest cuts of meat were sent to the lord's kitchens for consumption by his family and guests. The less desirable entrails or 'humbles' (sometimes known as umbles) were given to the huntsmen and servants by way of payment.

The servants of Sir William Petre at Ingatestone Hall certainly appreciated the taste of umble pie. Records kept at the hall show that on Christmas Day 1551, when local people and tenants from the estate joined Lord Petre's staff for dinner, two 'umble pasties' were among the dishes brought to the table. Umble pie was a mixture of heart, liver, kidney and tougher pieces of deer, with a pastry top. The expression 'eating humble pie', meaning to accept humiliation, probably arose from this medieval dining custom of feeding the lower orders. Samuel Pepys mentions the dish in his diary on 5 July 1662.

In centuries past, the term 'Essex calf' was a humorous term given not to a piece of beef, but as a nickname for anyone who came from Essex. The term was coined by Aphra Behn (1640-1689), an amazing woman for her times, who wrote Restoration comedies and was recruited by Charles II to act as a spy in Antwerp during the Dutch wars. 'Essex lions' was another nickname but this time it was given to Essex cattle when they arrived in the London markets, as they were of such sturdy stock.

Beef is still a favourite Sunday joint in Essex and we have an intriguing legend as to how the name 'beef sirloin' was created. With Epping Forest so close to London's seat of power, for centuries English monarchs enjoyed hunting there. After a very successful day's hunting in the forest, King James I returned to Friday Hill House at Chingford and was in high spirits. A wonderful banquet awaited him and as he caught sight of the splendid beef joint in the centre of the table, he declared that it deserved a title. Raising his sword in mock solemnity, James dubbed the meat 'Sir Loin of Beef. Arise Sir Loin'. Thereafter, the oak banquet table was carefully preserved and bore a brass plate with the inscription: 'All lovers of roast beef will like to be informed that on this table a loin was knighted by King James I on his return from hunting in Epping

Ingatestone Hall.

Forest.' However, this story is also claimed by Chingford's Pimp Hall, Epping's Copped Hall and the Spotted Dog Inn at Upton, West Ham, as well as other manor houses in other parts of England.

Bird Lore

Olivier de Serres, in his book on agriculture and husbandry published in 1600, wrote:

> No man need ever have an ill-provisioned house if there be but attached to it a dovecot, a warren and a fishpond. Herein meat may be found as readily at hand as if it were stored in a larder. Certainly a vast pigeon pie is a most useful standing dish in a country house for members of the family.

In Essex, culinary references to the pigeon in early medieval times show that it was not only a delicacy but made a regular appearance on the menu at court and in monasteries, as well as at farmers' tables. A fourteenth-century cookery book gives a recipe for stewed pigeons: 'Take peions and stop them with garlec pylled and gode hebres.' At that time, the birds were often roasted on spits and carefully sewn up at each end to prevent the much-prized gravy from escaping.

From all accounts, wild birds were plentiful. Country dwellers living among wildlife in the not too distant past have always sought to keep 'pest' species under a degree of control. Rooks, magpies, starlings, plovers, blackbirds and dunlin, even

An old dovecote.

tiny sparrows, were once shot or netted, usually by young boys, and used for pies and puddings. In Essex, and probably in surrounding counties, there was the old festival day celebrated on 12 May – for rook shooting. The backbone of the rook had to be removed or the meat would have an unpleasant taste.

With the introduction, from 1954, of parliamentary legislation covering the protection of birds, certain wild birds cannot now be killed unless they are proved to be a nuisance to crops:

> Sing a song of sixpence, a pocketful of rye
> Four and twenty blackbirds baked in a pie.

The Essex Pig

In the last few centuries, in the days before mass-produced food, Essex cottagers and many farm workers were able to provide for themselves. Although most of them were tied to their employers, who owned the land on which they farmed, they appear to have been self-sufficient, using their food reserve wisely. Nothing was wasted.

The family pig was important and was considered an insurance against the forthcoming winter. So it was looked after carefully throughout the year, growing fat on potatoes and greens grown in the plot behind the cottage. In the autumn, it was turned loose in neighbouring woodland to root out acorns, windfall fruit and grain left in the fields after harvest. This is an ancient custom known as pannage and existed in places around England; it continued in Epping Forest until the twentieth century. When the weather turned cold and winter approached, the pig was usually so fat that it had trouble walking and it was time for the killing:

> And he that can rear up a pig in his house
> Hath cheaper his bacon and sweeter his souse [salted meat].

Old almanacs suggest the traditional time for pig killing was around Hallontide, 11 November, so that there would be bacon, brawn and soused meat for Christmas. An Essex rhyme goes:

> At Michaelmas safely go stie up thy boar
> Lest straying abrode, you see him no more;
> The sooner the better for Hallontide nie;
> And better he brawneth if hard he do lie.

Many superstitious beliefs were attached to this auspicious event. For example, it was believed unlucky to look the pig in the eye when slaughtering it. Killing the pig was a messy business but it was essential, as the family that could not kill its pig

The famous Essex pig.

would very likely starve. Every part of the pig was used: the flitches of bacon were carefully salted and smoked, hams were carefully hung high in the rafters, and the head, trotters, offal, blade bones and spare ribs were all used. Sausages, faggots, black pudding and brawn (sometimes known as 'head cheese') were made and the pig's lard was rendered down and stored for the coming months. Everything was consumed – except the pig's squeal.

Arthur Young, in his *General View of the Agriculture of Essex* (1813), described the 'Essex half black' breed at Felix Hall, Kelvedon, owned by Charles Western MP, as 'the finest breed of hogs that I have seen in Essex, and indeed equal, if not superior to any elsewhere to be found'. At the beginning of the nineteenth century, agriculture still occupied about twice as many Essex households as all other industries put together. Western's championing of farming interests is believed to have helped him win elevation to the House of Lords in 1833.

Our world-famous breed, the Essex pig, almost passed into extinction during the 1960s but was saved by just one Essex-based farmer. The Essex pig is now classed as a rare breed and there are only fifty left worldwide. Great efforts on the part of the young farmer Jimmy Doherty at Pannington Hall Farm are being made to increase his herd of fifteen pure Essex pigs.

Our Daily Bread

Ceres, the goddess of corn and harvests, was worshipped by the Romans and it is from her name that we derive our English word 'cereal'. She was believed to watch over the growth of corn and the harvest. In Ancient Rome, the festival of

Cerealia, lasting for eight days, was once celebrated every April. It is believed that sacrifices were made to Ceres by the pagan population.

There is much superstition surrounding bread, still the staple nourishment of most Essex communities. The county has always been a fertile, agricultural one, with plentiful supplies of wheat and grain. Primitive man probably discovered that pounding coarse meal or grain, adding water and baking the resulting dough near an open fire created the first bread. Essex has long been the breadbasket of England, with its combination of rich soil and ideal farming conditions, growing grain right on the doorstep of the London markets. Lynn Pewsey, in *A Taste of Essex*, wrote:

> Breadmaking, of course, began in prehistoric times when grain was pounded together between two stones, moistened, formed into a dough and shaped and baked on very hot, flat stones, pulled from the fire. Later, it became apparent that if they were placed in an oven the heat could be conserved better and more bread made. These first ovens were fuelled by wood and that method of using wood, or more particularly brushwood, to fire the ovens has endured to modern times in Essex. Many older houses in the countryside have a lean-to at the rear or an outbuilding known as the 'back'us' (bake-house) where a fortnight's bread was baked at one go; the dough was kneaded in a kneading trough, which, when not in use, was used to store the flour.

Strange-sounding gadgets were used in bread-making. A bush fork was an instrument like a horseshoe on the end of a long iron rod, which was used to push the faggots (or tids) into the oven. A rastler was an elm pole used to pack the firewood into the oven.

Being the staple nourishment of many Essex farming folk, whose living also depended on successful corn harvests, bread has attracted many religious and pagan superstitions along the way, particularly within church rituals and folklore narratives. The 'host' or consecrated bread of the Eucharist is crucial to this important service. Many people consider it unlucky to throw away even stale bread, believing that if they do, they are destined to go hungry. To throw bread into the fire is said to be feeding the Devil. Corn gods once figured highly among pagan divinities worshipped by rural communities. Marking loaves with a cross during bread-making was an old Essex custom that continued well into the twentieth century. Some said it was to stop the Devil sitting on it.

Watermills to grind the grain for bread were mentioned in the Domesday Book, and there is much folklore connected with both the water and the grinding of corn and wheat. Before the Romans invaded, the native Britons used querns – large, flat circular stones – for grinding corn by hand. By the seventeenth and eighteenth centuries, virtually every village in Essex boasted its own windmill. There are still twenty-two windmills to be seen in the county, thanks to the many hardworking windmill preservation societies.

Surely one of the most magical moments in baking legend was Louis Pasteur's discovery of the wonders of yeast fermentation and how to make heavy dough rise to be light and digestible. No one until then knew exactly why the dough miraculously rose, seemingly by itself. Most people accepted it was just a spontaneous phenomenon rather than the simplicity of allowing micro-organisms of the fungi spores a chance to multiply. Another fortunate moment in food folklore must have been when a cook took an odd piece of dough, rounded and flattened it and maybe added fruit or honey, and the teacake made its debut into gastronomic folklore history.

The Essex huffer (or huffkin) is made from a 2lb piece of bread dough, which is flattened and cut into eight triangular pieces. The name is almost certainly derived from 'huff', a puff of wind, which is descriptive of its lightness. Older residents of North Essex, around Berden, Henham and Manuden, remember huffers and there is evidence that bakers in Barking and Dagenham's Old Village produced them in the early years of the twentieth century. Huffers are best split and eaten with butter.

In Clavering and surrounding villages, crickneys (also known as scrap buns or scritling cakes) were popular during Victorian times. They were small rolls made with pork fat and spice, and had a golden appearance. Pads or paddles were fat little loaves with very crusty bottoms, due to being cooked on the oven base. These loaves could be found in the Hanningfields area and around Chelmsford. Dannicks were a kind of Essex bread baked in some of the larger houses and small bakers around the Colchester area; they are now just a memory. Wholemeal flour was used in the recipe, and therefore they were a much denser, heavier bread. Legend tells us that the name derives from the Danes' arrival on the shores of England in the early eleventh century.

Magical Salt

Essential to human life, salt had a vital place in the country kitchen, the dairy and the medicine chest, as well as in the fishing industry, where, in the days before refrigeration, it preserved the catch. Much superstition is linked with salt, that precious commodity which has, since Celtic times, been extracted from seawater along the Essex coast. Lynn Pewsey, in *A Taste of Essex*, wrote:

> The remains of this industry can be seen in the form of the Red Hills that dot the shoreline still. These Red Hills were the sites of salt extraction; seawater was boiled in large earthenware tanks until the salt crystallised. Over many years the crystallising sites built up with earth and burnt debris to form mounds of reddish soil. Coastal salt extraction in Essex continued in Saxon and medieval times; the Domesday

Book recorded 52 'salt pans' in Essex. With the exception of one at Wanstead, these were all concentrated in the Tendring Hundred and along the north coast of the Blackwater. There were likely to have been many more unrecorded, particularly in the Dengie and Rochford Hundreds. Some place-names also record the salt-making industry, such as Salcott, which means 'the place where salt is stored'.

The discovery of salt, vital to the maintenance of life in its almost magical properties of food preservation, has been highly valued for many centuries. Roman soldiers and workers were often paid in salt – a salarium, from where we get the word 'salary'. The most commonly observed superstition concerning salt in modern times is the assumption that evil spirits are roused when salt is accidentally spilt – in some areas it is said that a tear will be shed for every grain scattered. The tossing of a pinch of the spilt salt over the left shoulder is regarded as an antidote to any ill luck, in the belief that it will drive away the Devil. Salt is reputed to have considerable power as a protective against evil influences. A little salt held in the palm of a woman giving birth is said to be of great benefit to mother and child. One superstition in the kitchen is that too much salt in the food is sometimes interpreted as a sign that the cook is in love.

The tradition of crystallising salt from seawater continues at the famous Maldon Crystal Salt Co., founded in 1882 on the site of a twelfth-century salt extraction works. This salt has a huge and successful market worldwide.

Sweetmeats

Colchester became well known for its local delicacy, candied eryngo, a sweetmeat which is made from the roots of the sea holly, *Eryngium maritimum*. This once grew in abundance along the Essex coast. Robert Buxton, a Colchester apothecary, established the eryngo trade, which became very successful in the seventeenth century. The candied sweetmeats – sometimes referred to as kissing comfits, as they were believed to have aphrodisiac properties – were presented to visiting royalty in Colchester. The most famous occasion was when, in August 1761, Princess Charlotte of Mecklenburgh-Strelitz was entertained in Colchester en route from Harwich to marry George III. The event was reported by the *London Gazette*:

> About five o'clock she came to Colchester and stopped at the house of Mr Enew, where she was received and waited upon by Mrs Enew and Mrs Ribow ... Mr Great of Colchester had the honour of presenting to her Majesty, while she was at Mr Enew's house, a box of candied eringo-root.

Eryngo roots, boiled or roasted, taste rather like chestnuts. When candied, they have a liquorice flavour. The Greeks are supposed to have eaten the stem and root, which they boiled or ate raw. Although candied eryngo root was no longer made commercially after 1865, in Colchester the recipe has been preserved and a label on a box in the Holly Trees Museum reads 'Eringo Roots Candyed and sold by Charles Great in the Old Twisted Posts and Pots in Colchester'.

Alcohol

> Wine is a very necessary thing in most families, and it is often spoiled by mismanagement of putting together. For if you let it stand too long before you get it cold, and do not take great care to put your barm upon it in time it summer beams, and blinks in the tub, so that it makes your wine fret.
> From the eighteenth-century *Essex Domestic Cookery Book*.

Alcohol has always played its part in feasts and festivals. Although the Romans in Essex were known to have planted vines 1,000 years earlier, it was following the arrival of the Normans in 1066 that wine-making flourished again in Essex. When facts and figures were being collected for the Domesday Book in 1086, there were already nine vineyards established. One of the most productive belonged to Sweyn FitzWymarc in Rayleigh; it yielded over 2,000 gallons of wine in a good summer.

The Saxons fermented honey to make mead, which their kings drank from silver-edged mazers. There were many different mead varieties, including metheglin and melomel. Hyppocras, a honey-based wine often served hot and flavoured with cinnamon, sunflower seeds, ginger and pepper, was much in vogue in medieval England. In *The Canterbury Tales*, Chaucer wrote of one of his characters:

> He drinkest ipocras, claree and vernage, Of spyces hote, t'encresen his corage.

Even today, many people enjoy making mead if they have access to large amounts of honey. At the Essex Amateur Winemaking Federation, the annual mead trophy is presented to the best exhibit of mead.

For centuries, Essex folk drank ale produced by maltsters and brewsters. The lady of the house – the ale wife – seems to have been proficient at the craft. Often she carried on the brewing business after her husband died, using methods still familiar today. She used malted barley (germinated and roasted), water and yeast, often flavoured with herbs or nettles. Because the boiling process killed off bacteria, ale was less dangerous to drink than water. A second fermentation produced a less alcoholic drink known as small beer, which was considered to be far more healthy and was given to children to drink. Ale was originally distinguished from beer, which was brewed in the same way but with the addition of hops, which not only gave beer its bitter taste but more importantly acted as a preservative.

The strength of ale was important. Many Essex innkeepers feared a visit from the ale-conner. He was the dreaded inspector of ales, appointed by the manorial authorities, whose job it was to call on innkeepers when a new batch of ale was ready for sale. In earlier centuries, it was tradition to set out a bush or 'pole' of ivy once a new brew was ready. The ale-conner, wearing sturdy leather breeches, would pay an unannounced visit to the inn and demand a jug of ale. He would pour some of the ale onto a wooden bench and then sit in the puddle he'd made. There he would stay drinking for a while, but would be careful not to change his position. At the end of the testing time, he would rise from his seat. If the liquor was impure and the sugar had not been properly fermented, the ale-conner's leather breeches would stick to the bench. However, if the brew was well fermented, the ale-conner would be able to rise easily – proof of a good, strong ale. The punishment for selling bad ale or knowingly giving inaccurate measurements could be an hour or so in the village stocks. The old method of assessing the quality of the brew continued in Essex inns until hydrometers and technological brewing improvements made the job more accurate – and certainly less messy.

Inn signs have been the subject of song and story ever since 1540, when each innkeeper was ordered to hang out a sign or forfeit his livelihood:

> Hops, Reformation, bays and beer,
> Came in to England all in one year.

It was the Flemish weavers fleeing from the Low Countries in the sixteenth

The old ale-conner.

century who introduced the cultivated hop which was being used by French brewers to preserve and flavour their ales. They came to Braintree, Coggeshall, Weathersfield, Colchester and the surrounding towns and villages. Although hops grew wild in our countryside, there was a cultivated hop garden at Ingatestone Hall which was doubtless used by Lord Petre's own brewer, who in one year made at least thirty-two brewings. Each brewing filled thirty-two kilderkins (barrels), each holding 18 gallons, at a total cost of £75.

William Cobbett, the eighteenth-century writer who often visited Essex, had very definite ideas about drinking beer. He preferred it to the newfangled tea, which he despised:

> The drink, which has come to take the place of beer, has, in general, been tea. It is notorious, that tea has no useful strength in it; that it, besides being good for nothing, has badness in it, because it is well-known to produce want of sleep in many cases, and in all cases, to shake and weaken the nerves.
>
> William Cobbett, *Cottage Economy* (1821)

The Weald of Kent produced hops for 400 years and was considered to be the finest place in England in which to grow hops. But just after the Second World War, when some of the Kentish farmers' hop fields became infested with a virulent hop disease, an Essex farmer, Robert Goodchild, was asked to experiment with growing hops at Codham Hall Farm at Great Warley. Robert planted several thousand cuttings of Fuggles hops on a 2-acre paddock near his farm, on the hillside facing south, now part of the M25 motorway. Backed by

Farmer Robert Goodchild and his family in his hop field.

Above: Essex hop pickers, 1954.

Left: Hops are still grown in Essex Gardens.

the Hop Marketing Board and Whitbread's, Robert's efforts produced more than 5,000 bushels. He won two major awards at the Brewers' Exhibition at Olympia in 1954 and 1957, competing against Kentish growers. Robert's success with hop-growing entered him in the annals of farming folklore.

Essex beer has always had a good reputation and has been brewed by Ridley's at Hartford End since 1842. The other old county breweries have gone, even the huge Ind Coope brewery at Romford. Gray's have kept their forty-nine pubs in Essex, although their once lovely old brewery at Chelmsford has been transformed into a shopping complex. There are some small firms brewing beer, most notably Crouch Vale at South Woodham Ferrers and John Boyce's Mighty Oak at Maldon.

SIX

CURIOSITIES

They were strange and wonderful things...
Thomas Traherne (1637-1674)

Every county has something special about it – legends, customs and those extraordinary little places unique to that particular part of the country. Essex presents many faces to the world, with its mixture of large towns, villages and coastal resorts. Many are well known and well exploited for the tourist trade, but nestling quietly in nooks and crannies of the Essex countryside are many odd, unexpected and curious treasures with an interesting tale to tell.

The Magic of Stones

Before the birth of the study of geology, people must have had an explanation for some of the strange features found in the Essex landscape. Across the county, there are many unusual stones to be found, both large and small. As a child, Kathleen Curtis in Colchester was given a penny by the local farmer for every bucketful of stones she collected from the field. Other farmers believed that there was no real point in collecting stones, as the land would 'only grow more'. One tale tells of a Colchester farmer whose old uncle kept a 'mother-stone' on his window sill, believing that pebbles were its offspring.

Essex has many puddingstones, so-called because they resemble giant plum puddings, containing small browny-red pebbles like currants. They were once believed to be imbued with magical and medicinal powers. Technically known as conglomerates, they vary in size from a few centimetres across to about 2m and resemble concrete. When Pope Gregory's missionaries attempted to convert the pagan Britons to Christianity in AD 596, the holy brothers did all they could to

A Colchester farmer and his wife in 1880.

discourage devilish stone worship, yet superstition has lingered on in some parts of the county even today.

Large stones were often built into the base of churches, such as those at Broomfield, Fyfield, Dunmow and North Stifford. A line of boulders stretches from the river Lea towards Epping Upland, Marks Tey, Waltham Abbey and Ugley Green. Some believe the stones were used as markers by the early tribes of East Anglia.

An interesting story surrounds the huge stone found in the churchyard at St Botolph's at Beauchamp Roding. In centuries past, when the villagers started building the church, they chose a site near the village, dragging down the huge stone that had stood on top of the hill. Next morning it had gone and was back on top of the hill. Undaunted, the stalwarts dragged it down again, only to find it back on top of the hill. After this had happened for the third time, the villagers gave in to divine intervention and built the church on the hilltop.

Ancient stones gave their names to some local towns and villages. For example, Leytonstone means 'the stone at Leyton'. In 1780, Philip Morant wrote: 'On the road to Epping is Leyton Stone, most probably from one of the Roman military stones placed there.' Alphamstone near Colchester probably takes its name from the large stone built into the west wall of the nave of St Catherine's church, which is believed to date back to the Bronze Age. There is also Ingatestone, whose great

Above left: The mysterious Beauchamp Roding stone.

Above right: The stone at Leytonstone.

Ancient stones at Ingatestone.

stone or boulder was brought down during the last Ice Age and is now split into two pieces which are positioned at the junction of Fryerning Lane and the High Street. A large stone which can be seen at Newport is known as the Leper Stone. Some believe it was the spot where villagers left food for the lepers; others say that it was used for cleaning coins that might have been handled by the lepers before being passed to the stallholders of the market nearby. The cleansing water was contained in the hollow top of the stone.

Churches

> I like that ancient Saxon phrase, which calls the burial ground God's Acre.
> (Longfellow)

The ceremony and rituals surrounding the burial of the dead are fascinating and give us an insight into the life and death of some of our forebears. Colchester Castle Museum has the tombstone of Marcus Favonius Facilis, believed to have been a member of the invading Roman army who died while serving at Colchester in the early years after the conquest.

Abbeys, priories and monasteries were the centre of religious life before churches were built. The first church buildings were erected by wealthy landowners, which

Colchester Castle.

Greensted church; the oldest wooden church in the world.

is one of the reasons why many churches were built relatively close to existing manor houses. Only priests were buried in the churchyard originally. The rich were encased in elaborate tombs within the church and the poor had to make do with a simple shroud and burial in a hole in the ground.

As land began to be used up for burial, charnel houses were built to store the redundant bones extracted from the churchyard. At the north-east corner of the churchyard at St Peter's church in Colchester, there is a charnel house built of brick, with a vaulted underground structure for depositing bones. Only the steps leading down to the entrance of the charnel house are now visible. It was built in the early sixteenth century, when the vestry above it was added to the church.

St Andrew's church at Greensted, near Ongar, has long been famous as Europe's oldest wooden building. That record still stands and research based on tree rings has dated the timbers to between 1063 and 1103 – a reminder that Norman buildings, like Saxon, were constructed mostly of wood.

Maiden's Garland

At St Michael's church in Theydon Mount, near Epping, hangs a maiden's garland. This eighteenth-century relic is part of the funerary custom practised when the deceased was an unmarried girl who was believed to have led an unblemished life. Often known as a virgin's crown or krans (meaning chaplet or wreath), it was made from rosettes of fine paper fixed to tiny wooden sticks that crossed each other at the top. Although the method of construction varied from village to village, a favoured technique in Essex was to fix the paper flowers to a circular wooden frame made from hazel or willow to resemble a crown. Suspended from the centre was a white paper glove or handkerchief. The name of the girl, her age and date of death was written thereon. After the funeral, the garland would be hung above the family pew or from a hook on a beam in the church.

Wanstead Watch

In Wanstead's church of the Virgin Mary, a large tombstone marks the burial vault of Sir Joseph Wilton, an eminent eighteenth-century sculptor, and his family. This is a Grade II listed tombstone which is meant to represent the entrance to the Holy Sepulchre at Jerusalem. Sir Joseph was a founder member of the Royal Academy. It is rumoured that the box was used by watchmen during the time when the resurrectionists were stealing newly buried corpses to sell to medical students or hospitals for research.

Hornchurch

On the eastern gable of the chancel of St Andrew's church at Hornchurch, built in 1391, a Highland bull's head of stone with copper horns is displayed. This is possibly the only one of its kind in England. Some historians say the emblem represents the ancient trade of currying and leather dressing connected with the village, whose main road was known as Pelt Street, with Tanner Street close by. In 1158, Henry II endowed a priory whose motherhouse was designated the Horned Monastery.

Wanstead church of the Virgin Mary, with its unusual monument.

St Andrew's church, Hornchurch, with its famous bull's head.

Philip Morant, the eighteenth-century Essex historian, suggested that the bull's head and horns may have been the crest of the religious house of Savoy, but this has not been verified. In the fourteenth century, the motif appeared on the Hornchurch priory seal but by this time the village had been known as 'Hornechirche' for over a century. Incredulity and sadness met the news that the famous bull's head had been stolen in July 1999 but with due ceremony a replacement was erected on the eastern gable in 2001.

Green Man

The symbol of the enigmatic green man can be found all around Essex. From Herongate to Little Braxted, the Green Man is one of the most popular pub signs in the county. He pops up in national folklore and many people delight in spotting his foliate face staring down from ancient buildings, water spouts, church doors and pews, carved ceilings and corbels. The term 'Green Man' was coined by Lady Raglan in 1939, when she included it in her article for the *Folklore Journal*. In *The Quest for the Green Man*, John Matthews writes:

> Green man has been with us for a long time. He has been worshipped, carved, painted and sculpted out of branches and ferns, praised, reviled, studied, filmed and sung about.

No one knows who this mysterious figure was. He has oak and vine leaves growing from his mouth, eyes and ears and sometimes camouflaging his entire face. Maybe he was the wood spirit so often referred to in folk tales – a John

The Green Man at Herongate.

Barleycorn character. He is always with us and has certainly been a favourite motif of woodcarvers and stonemasons for centuries.

The Green Man can be seen looking down from a roof boss in the timber-framed belfry of All Saints church at Stock. He is there at St Mary the Virgin church in Kelvedon, where he hides outside the west wall. At St Laurence church in Blackmore, there are two similar fourteenth-century Green Men with foliage framing their faces, and at St Giles church in Mountnessing, he stares out from a capital on the north aisle. He is there – everywhere.

Inscriptions

There are some interesting memorials in Essex churches. An inscription at Great Burstead churchyard seems to have been the favourite of many monumental masons:

> Remember man as you pass by,
> As you are now, so there was I,
> As I am now, so you must be,
> Therefore prepare to follow me.

After a later burial in the same plot, the following lines were added:

CURIOSITIES

> To follow you, I'm not content,
> Until I know which way you went.

It seems bizarre to find a connection to slavery in the quiet Essex countryside. However, in the corner of Little Parndon churchyard lies the grave of a black slave, Hester Woodley, who died on 13 May 1767, aged sixty-two. She was slave to Mrs Bridget Woodley, who on her death passed the ownership of the slave, together with her belongings, to her daughter. It is interesting to note that Hester bore her mistress's surname, a common practice in the days of slavery.

A gravestone bearing a rather odd inscription can be found at St Osyth churchyard. Although badly eroded, one can still decipher the most important part – the date:

> Here Lieth Ann The
> Wife of Will R
> Who Departed This Life 17th Day of Feb
> in ye year 1734/5

When using the old Julian calendar of pre-1752, it was customary to count the year from March to March. It was therefore common practice to add the next year to the tombstones of those who died in the month of February.

In the old churchyard at Pitsea Mount, near Basildon, a gravestone reads: 'Ann Freeman died 20 March 1879. Here lies a weak and sinful worm, the vilest of her race, saved through God's electing love, his free and sovereign grace'. What did this woman do to deserve such an epitaph? Answer: absolutely nothing. This is a traditional epitaph and not specific to Ms Freeman. It turns on the doctrine of original sin for which one is not personally responsible and from which one is redeemed by divine grace. Eighteenth-century hymn writers delighted in referring to human beings as worms – it comes from scripture: 'I am a worm and no man; a reproach of men and despised of the people.' (Psalms 22.6).

Bells

The subject of Essex bells conjures up many superstitions and legends. Bells have called people to prayer since the seventh century. William Addison, in his book *Essex Heyday*, states that during the reign of Queen Elizabeth I, there was a tradition of ringing the village church bells on the morning of her birthday, 7 September. They were also rung when the lord of the manor returned from service overseas, and even when he returned from the assizes at Chelmsford.

Essex churchwardens' account books are full of references to money left in wills to be paid to the bell-ringers for beer. Sometimes genial parishioners provided doles and payment for bell-ringing in their wills. The Revd Montagu

Benton records such a bequest made by a Saffron Walden mercer, Thomas Turner, in his will dated 10 June 1623. Twenty shillings annually were left for a memorial sermon on the anniversary of his burial, thirty-three shillings and fourpence to the bell-ringers and six shillings and eightpence to the parish clerk for preparing the bells for ringing.

All Saints church at Maldon initially housed a trio of bells. In 1699, they were replaced by six, although two more were added in 1922. The inscription on the old bells declares:

> When first this steeple three did hold
> They were the emblems of a scold
> No music then, but now shall see
> What pleasant music six shall be?

At Danbury, there is a well-known enduring legend concerning the Devil, who paid a visit to St John the Baptist church, high on the hill. The Devil stole the fifth bell from the belfry. This was the bell tolled to mark the passing of a soul. When the parishioners discovered the theft, they set up a 'hue and cry' and chased in hot pursuit of Old Nick, who promptly dropped the bell, whereupon it rolled down to a place still known as Bell Hill Wood. Legend tells us that when the fifth bell was replaced, the vicar could find no local bell-ringer brave enough to ring it, in case the chime summoned the Devil to make a return visit.

An unusual tradition is carried out at the beautiful church of Great Bromley, where the hat of the captain of the bell-ringers is dated and hung beneath the tower in the belfry on his death. No one knows when this ritual began but one of the hats is dated 1716.

Timekeeping

The old town hall, church and village clocks seem to tick on, taking life in their stride. As centuries slipped by, the old hand-forged timepieces were replaced with more modern mechanisms. We can, however, still see some beautiful examples of the county's clocks at Tymperleys Clock Museum in Colchester, which has some of the finest collections from the seventeenth, eighteenth and nineteenth centuries.

At Little Burstead's Stockwell Hall, once a moated farmhouse and later the Essex seat of the Earls of Mexborough, there is an eighteenth-century bellcote and, below the gable, a large clock face with a single hand and figures said to be made of blackened bones. At Ingatestone Hall, a lovely eighteenth-century, blue enamelled, one-handed clock can be seen. It bears the motto 'Sans Dieu Rien' ('Without God, nothing').

Curiosities

Above: Little Burstead's Stockwell Hall, with its clock figures of blackened bones.

Right: Ingatestone Hall, with its one-handed clock.

One of the county's oldest clocks can be found built into the south tower of the parish church of St Leonard-at-the-Hythe. The clock face of stone dates back to 1500 and its circular dial has radiating figures and carved spandrels. Mavis Sipple, in her book *Extraordinary Essex*, writes:

> Before the days of clocks and watches, one simple way to record the passing of time was by using an hourglass. Similar to a giant egg timer they were often found in churches, resting in a wrought iron stand fixed near the pulpit. The hourglass would help the preacher gauge the length of his sermon. When the sand ran out, he knew he had been preaching for an hour and would often up-end the glass and start again.

A preacher would be known as a two-hour or a three-hour man or even a six-hour man. Most of these hourglasses have become broken or lost, but occasionally the wrought iron stand can be found near the pulpit.

There are now just a few of these hourglasses to be seen around Essex. One ancient hourglass was cherished at the church of St Edmund at Abbess Roding until it was stolen during the 1990s. All that remains is the wrought-iron stand.

Colchester's Water Tower

Colchester folk named their newly-built water tower Jumbo when it was opened on 27 September 1883. Jumbo was the 6½-ton African elephant who, with his mate Alice, was one of the most popular animals living at London Zoo in the nineteenth century. When Phineas Taylor Barnum, the American manager of 'The Greatest Show on Earth' bought Jumbo for his circus, there was a huge public outcry from thousands of English elephant-fanciers, including Queen Victoria, and many telegrams were sent to Barnum by the editor of the *Morning Post* enquiring on what terms he would return Jumbo. Barnum replied that with 50 million Americans awaiting his arrival, £100,000 could not stop the purchase. Protest songs were composed, to no avail. Jumbo became Barnum's chief attraction and when he died he was stuffed and exhibited in the Barnum Museum of Natural History in the US. Colchester's Jumbo still stands but plans are afoot to convert it to living accommodation.

The Jumbo water tower at Colchester.

Romany Burial

It was once against Romany tradition to be buried in a churchyard although there are Romany burial grounds at Strethall in Essex, which were used by the Dymock, Gray and Shaw families. Some Romany families preferred to bury their dead at the place where they died, close to a hedge or wall – hence the East Anglian expression 'lying by the wall' to describe someone who is dead. A century ago, the custom was to burn the gypsy's caravan (*vardo*) when the man of the family died. Their treasured crockery was strewn at the place where they were buried. Often a thorn bush was planted on the grave, as a marker and spirit plant.

Doors and Devils

Essex has many strange legends concerning church doors. At St Mary's church in Runwell, near Wickford, there is a burnt-in impression of a great clawlike hand on the inside of the south door, which is said to be the hand mark of the Devil. The story tells of Rainaldus, the parish curate, who was conducting a service when the Devil made a grab for him. The terrified curate escaped through the south door while the Devil, unable to pass through the sanctified portals, angrily

A gypsy *vardo*.

burned his mark into the old oak door. The congregation dispersed and came back later but their curate had disappeared. On the spot where he had been standing was a puddle of green liquid, which was bubbling by the south porch. In this pool lay a small stone resembling a human head. Later, this was mounted on the south wall near where Rainaldus held that last Mass. It bears the Latin inscription '*Stipendia peccatimors*' (The wages of sin is death). Next time you attend a baptism service, look around the church and note how the north door is, where possible, left open. This is so that, at the words 'renounce the devil and all his works', Satan can leave unhindered.

Several myths surround the small Saxon church of St Botolph's at Hadstock, seven miles north of Saffron Walden. The church has the oldest door in regular use in Britain. The legend revolves around St Botolph, who began a small monastery in the kingdom of East Anglia. He is believed to be buried in the church grounds. In 1144, the monks of Ely referred to Hadstock as 'that place sanctified to religion in days of old by the Holy Botolph, there at rest'.

Although cattle hide was often placed between the church door and the hinges to protect the wood, when the door of St Botolph's church was removed for repair, the skin beneath the hinge was found to be human. As flailing was a punishment at the time, the skin might possibly be that of a Dane caught plundering the church.

Fire

Once commonplace on many buildings, firemarks can still be found on the front of some houses in Essex. Many people believe that the Great Fire of London in 1666 laid the foundations for organised firefighting. Wooden houses gave way to brick buildings and owners began to insure them against fire. Insurance companies realised their losses would be limited if they employed men to put out fires in the buildings for which they provided cover. The buildings were identified by lead or copper badges or 'firemarks', which showed which company insured them. The Essex Equitable Insurance Society was founded in Colchester in 1802 and was one of the first to equip its volunteer firemen with uniforms and a firecart. Later, steam engines were introduced.

An early fire brigade was started in Brentwood in 1886. James Fair and a few other part-time men were the first officers. James continued for fifty years, becoming the longest-serving fireman in Britain. When a fire was reported, James would summon his officers using his bugle, and they would round up any spare horses to pull the firecart. During his time, James served under six fire chiefs and is thought to have attended hundreds of fires in this once small agricultural town.

Just around the time James Fair was born, the chaplain of Brentwood, the Revd Francis Rhodes, narrowly escaped death in a blaze that had broken out in the High Road bakery. Bravely he leapt on to the roof to try to stop the fire from spreading to

CURIOSITIES

Right: A firemark.

Below: James Fair (standing at the front on the right), a Brentwood fireman who was fifty years in service.

James Fair (standing at the front on the far right) with his team outside the fire station, 1910.

adjoining buildings. Five years later, his son Cecil was born. Had Francis perished in the fire, the history of Africa and the British Empire could have been very different.

Curious Bones

Whalebone Lane in Dagenham is believed to derive its name from the famous pair of whalebones which once stood at the entrance to the old Whalebone House in Chadwell Heath. The house was demolished after being bombed during the Second World War and the bones – which were believed to be rib bones from a whale that had been stranded in the Thames in 1658 (the year of Oliver Cromwell's death) – were mounted on either side of the Barking and Dagenham Museum at Valence House. When the museum was renovated during the 1980s, the whalebones were taken down and are now stored in the cellar.

Nine Men's Morris

Tangible traces of leisure activities through the ages are generally both rare and diverse. An ancient carving of a board for playing the ancient game of Nine Men's Morris can be found on the windowsill of St John the Baptist church at Finchingfield. The board is made up of three concentric squares and is known to

Nine Men's Morris at Finchingfield.

have been played by two people with nine counters each. The object was to get three counters in a row and to capture all opposing pieces. The game has been carved in other places around the world, including the deck of a Viking ship in Norway, the steps of the Acropolis in Athens and on a Roman tile dug up in Silchester. Shakespeare wrote in *A Midsummer Night's Dream*:

> The Nine Mens Morris is fill'd up with mud
> And the quaint mazes in the wanton green
> For lack of tread are indistinguishable.

Dene Holes

Over the centuries, many strange stories have evolved around the collection of deep holes sunk into the chalky ground of Hangman's Wood at East Thurrock. These circular pits are known as Dene Holes and go down at least 50ft. Tunnels that are about 20ft long are linked to the shafts. Some experts have said they are merely chalk quarries from Celtic times. Some people firmly believe they were hiding places for villagers from the time of the Danish raids on Thurrock; others feel they were used merely as grain storage places. They may have been there for 1,000 years – the mystery has never been solved.

HMS *Beagle*

During its five-year scientific expedition from 1831 to 1836, the Admiralty research vessel HMS *Beagle* was home to the eminent naturalist Charles Darwin.

The ship was launched in 1820 at Woolwich Royal Dockyard. Under the command of Captain Robert Fitzroy, Darwin and his assistants sailed around the world, researching the fauna, flora and geology of many countries. This equipped Darwin for his later investigations, which were condensed within his great work, *The Origin of the Species*, published in 1859.

Following the expedition, HMS *Beagle* was of no further use to the Admiralty. It was taken over by the coastguard and became a watch vessel with permanent moorings on the river Roach near Paglesham. The crew was deployed to prevent smuggling, which was rife in this part of the Essex coast. In 1870, the decision came to break up the *Beagle* for scrap but first the useful timbers, with their distinctive carpenter markings, were recovered and used in the construction of local barns and houses. Today, the occupants of those riverside buildings are probably unaware of the part their house timbers played in British history. Meanwhile, remains of the *Beagle*, including its giant anchor, have recently been discovered at Potton Island, the former home of the Atomic Weapons Research Establishment, which lies opposite Paglesham. It is hoped that a memorial stone will be commissioned to mark the spot.

Underground

A rural bungalow nestling in the Kelvedon Hatch countryside, just twenty miles from Westminster, covered a very big secret when the site was acquired by the Government in the early 1950s during the Cold War with the Soviet Union. Myths and suppositions were rife and the local people, although not knowing exactly what it was, nicknamed it the Hole in the Ground. The 100ft-deep bunker contained rooms for up to 600 'key personnel', a BBC studio, dormitories, electricity generators and its own water supply, all within 21,000 square feet. At first it served as an operations centre for Fighter Command then, from the 1960s, as the emergency seat of national government in the event of a nuclear war. Thankfully the bunker – like many of the defences of past centuries – was never used in anger and it has, for the past decade, become a tourist attraction.

Emerging Essex Customs

When does custom become folklore? Traditional life and death and the living in between are covered in one form or another. Many of the everyday things we say and do are linked to bygone times. Some traditions have been resurrected ostensibly for the tourist market. New forms of folklore are being created in different ways, such as tying a bunch of balloons to a gate or door to indicate the location of a children's party, creating a wayside shrine to someone who has lost their life in a motoring accident, or attaching photographs and toys to children's graves.

Seven

Phenomena

> ...like one in dread who speeds through the recesses of some haunted pile and dares not look behind.
>
> Percy Bysshe Shelley (1792-1822)

From the numerous ghost books concentrated on Essex, interest seems to be increasing in matters supernatural, although there has always been a strong seam of ghostly tales. In our modern, brightly-lit county, there is a strange paradox in our thinking about phantoms: we deny their existence and at the same time we are afraid of them. Even people who have seen or heard something for which there is apparently no natural explanation sometimes continue to remain unconvinced about the world of the ghosts.

There is no need to look hard for spirits in Essex; the place is so full of echoes of the past that the stories come up in normal conversation. Local folklore abounds with references to legendary black dogs, grey and white ladies, benevolent kindly spirits, unexplained phenomena, poltergeists and, in some cases, fairly grim and malevolent monk manifestations. Darren Mann, a ghost sleuth who manages the Paranormal Database and has investigated much of the occult activity and poltergeist tales that have come his way, reckons Essex to be one of the most haunted counties in England.

There appears to be a widespread notion that the dead can reveal their presence to the living and that some people are better than others at perceiving them. So, many of the folk tales are connected with churches and graveyards in the county.

Borley Rectory

The village of Borley on the Essex/Suffolk border became famous almost overnight in the late 1920s, when Borley Rectory was described as 'the most

Borley Rectory in 1929.

haunted house in England'. It has inspired more books to be written about psychical research than any other place in the world.

Borley Rectory was built by the Reverend Henry Dawson Ellis Bull in 1863, on the site of an ancient house. Soon after Henry moved in, he and his family felt that they were not alone. Some of his fourteen children became nervous when a woman dressed in a nun's habit was seen peering through the dining room window. Henry promptly had the window bricked up but there were many such incidents recorded in his diaries. Whispers were heard around the house, accompanied by footsteps and tappings, and one of Henry's daughters was woken up one night by a slap on her face, although there was no one in the room. Several people reported seeing a strange woman walking along the path, which was later named Nun's Walk, and others had seen a tall dark man in the grounds, who promptly disappeared when he was spoken to.

In 1892, Henry died and the house passed to his son Harry. Within weeks, Henry's ghost was seen at the rectory. Servants' bells often rang when no member of the family had pulled the bell cord. The most persistent feature were the strange heavy footsteps which always seemed to occur at times when there was no one in those parts of the house from which the sounds appeared to come. Harry developed a keen interest in the afterlife and promised jokingly that he would try to make contact after his death. He planned to throw mothballs about 'so that you will know it is me', but there are no accounts of Harry's return in any form.

The next incumbent was the Revd Eric Smith, who took up residence with his wife Mabel in October 1928. Mrs Smith was worried about the continuing curious incidents that were taking place at Borley and contacted the *Daily Mirror*, who printed a sensational article which brought the psychic investigator Harry Price to the village. During Price's investigations, mysterious footsteps, whispering and the ringing of bells were regularly heard, accompanied by what he called 'poltergeist activity'. Vases were smashed as they dropped to the floor and candlesticks hurled themselves down the stairs. Keys shot out of their locks in the doors. This was too much for the Smiths and they left Borley in April 1930.

On 16 October 1930, the Revd Lionel Foyster – a cousin of Harry Bull – moved into the rectory with his wife Marianne. During the five years they lived at Borley, the psychic phenomena increased. Messages appeared on walls, addressed to Marianne, pleading for 'Mass, Light and Prayers'. Marianne also saw the ghost of Henry Bull. One night as she was passing the bathroom, she was hit in the face by an object – she knew not what – and the wound bled for a long time. The following night, as the Foysters lay in bed, several objects, including a hammer head and cotton reels, were hurled at them. The couple left in 1935.

Harry Price wrote several books about Borley Rectory, which eventually mysteriously burned down in February 1939. Lights were often seen in the ruins before they were demolished in 1943. When the site was cleared, part of a skull, believed to be a woman's, was found at the site, together with church ornaments.

Romford

There are more sceptics in the world of newspapers than in any other walk of life. So the idea of a ghost in an office inhabited by journalists would attract derision. Not so among those working at the former *Romford Times* offices at No. 2 High Street in the 1950s and '60s. Those who did not actually believe in its existence kept silent out of respect for those who claimed to have felt its presence or seen 'evidence' of its existence.

The property, which was one of the oldest houses in the ancient market town, had been converted by owners Wilson and Whitworth to include a stationery shop on the ground floor, with the editorial offices above. Stanley Wilson, grandson of the founder, was among the first to sense the ghost's presence on the top floor of the building. What he saw one night he would not reveal but he never again went up to that floor at night alone and refused to allow any stories to be written about it. Only after Stanley's death did the first story appear. By that time, the evidence had grown. Sports editor Don Hill had been working late one night alone, typing a report in the outer of the two rooms, when he saw the handle of the door to the inner room turn and the door open. There was no one there.

Another time, on a Saturday night, reporter Brian Potter was typing out results from the Dagenham Town Show he had just covered. It was a chilly evening and the old gas fire was on, when Brian suddenly felt a chill come over the room and what he later described as the sound of feet in canvas shoes shuffling across the floor from the darkened far corner of the room. The sound stopped between Brian and the fire and he felt the heat had suddenly been blocked off, as though there was someone standing there. The time was 10.40 p.m. Brian grabbed his belongings and fled.

It was precisely at the same time the following night that the editor, Joe Ellis, was working at his desk on the floor below when he heard the sound of footsteps on the stairs. He was alone in the building but it was not unusual for staff to wander in. All the reporters had keys so that they could complete their stories of the evening in time for sub-editing the following morning. Who was it who had just come up the stairs and opened the outer door to Joe's office? No one. The place was deserted.

One by one, the journalists were subjected to similar ghostly happenings, usually late at night. The old property was destined for demolition and an adjoining building became the temporary home of the newspaper. It was eventually revealed that a woman had hanged herself in the old building 300 years earlier, which may explain the hauntings. One peculiar additional recollection of Brian's was that the feet seemed to be moving 4in above the floor. It was discovered that No. 2 High Street, built without foundations only yards from the river Rom, had sunk 4in from the level of 300 years ago, settling slowly into the Romford mud.

When a new office block was built on the site, sceptics and believers alike waited for the return of the *Romford Times* office ghost. They were to be disappointed. If it had ever existed, it disappeared along with the rubble and hundreds of years of Romford history.

Peter Owen worked at the offices throughout the period of these stories but never experienced the ghost for himself:

> Not once, unless you want to count the time when I let myself in late one evening and saw someone go in the direction of the outside toilets. I thought I would also visit them before going upstairs to the reporters' room. I walked along the corridor in the same direction only to find the door at the end padlocked. I had been mistaken. I must have imagined the person walking ahead of me. I did, didn't I?

Warley

Down in the depths of the basement at the central office of the Ford Motor Co. in Warley, a ghostly spirit walks the endless corridors, manifesting himself from time to time to employees. Ken Marsh, a spiritual medium, has encountered the ghost:

> When I came to work at Central Office four years ago, I heard stories about people who had experienced brushes with the Warley ghost. I certainly felt the presence of a wandering spirit in the building. Those feelings were confirmed when I was walking along the basement corridor which leads to the receiving bay. The ghost

Ken Marsh, spirit medium, at the Ford Motor Co. in Warley.

of a soldier walked straight through me. It was such a strong manifestation that it virtually knocked me off balance. I didn't see a spiritual form, but I felt the visitation so strongly that I knew it was a man, and a soldier.

The building is on the site of the famous old Warley Barracks, erected in 1805, and there have been reports of manifestations of soldiers, usually in old-fashioned uniform. Ninety-five-year-old Jim Reddell, Chelsea Pensioner and first Freeman of the Borough of Brentwood, recalled:

> When I was stationed at Warley I casually mentioned the figure known as the 'Green Archer' who was often seen at the armament depot at Warley and the story certainly caused unnerving disturbance among the new recruits! There is another legend that a young soldier who, upon learning that he was to be posted to India, deserted. When arrested, he was brought back to the barracks where he hanged himself.

Gidea Park

The old gibbet at Gallows Corner in Gidea Park was in a dilapidated state during the eighteenth century. The local squire claimed the wood and ordered it to be made into a four-poster bed. When the village carpenter erected the bed in the squire's bedroom, the squire tested it and jokingly said, 'I'll sleep the sleep of the dead tonight.' His prediction came true: the next morning, he was found dead in the bed.

Ninety-five-year-old James Reddell, a Chelsea Pensioner who served at Warley Barracks.

Panfield

The Saxons called Panfield an area of 'open country on the banks of the river Pant'. No Saxon has been seen in spirit form but there was certainly an old lady haunting the Bell pub for many years before the present licensee took over. An exorcism was performed by the local vicar prior to the change of ownership. The spirit obviously liked the atmosphere, as she refused to go.

One day, when the landlord was cleaning out the fireplace in the lounge bar early in the morning with his Jack Russell, a sharp bang reverberated through the room although not a soul was there. The dog heard it too and reacted when a woman's voice was heard. Staff members have heard a child calling out when there were no children around. 'They're friendly ghosts so we don't mind them being around,' said Graham, the new licensee.

Basildon

When dealing with psychic phenomena, it is interesting to read about apparitions that suddenly make an appearance in places that have had no previous encounters with the paranormal. This happened in Basildon during the early 1960s, at the time when new houses and roads were being created on ancient land that is mentioned in the Domesday Book.

It was in the area around the sixteenth-century church of the Holy Cross that a red-robed figure – some described him as a monk – began to be seen around twilight. None of the older generation who had lived in that part of Basildon had ever seen or heard of a spectre of this sort before but it scared at least a dozen women (and some men) who worked at the Ford Tractor Plant and used Church Road as a short cut to their homes on the Fryerns Estate. Some became so terrified that they refused to use that route home.

The monk was seen to walk through solid objects near the church. It is thought that he was one of two rectors who were expelled and possibly murdered at the time of the Reformation. The ghost tale attracted several national newspapers, particularly when the curate of Holy Cross church, the Revd Bernard Lloyd, agreed to stage an all-night vigil. The date selected was 18 February 1964 and, as well as local journalists, there were photographers, a television crew and a reporter from the *Daily Mail*. The red monk failed to put in an appearance, probably unsettled by the television crew's lights, which illuminated the old church and graveyard. If nothing else, the story of the ghost succeeded in putting the 600-year-old church – one of the few remaining relics of pre-New Town Basildon – on the map. There was a reported sighting in 1972 but nothing further since.

Prittlewell

Some years ago, Simon Thwaites from Billericay often took a lunch break from his photographic course at Southend College to eat his lunch in Priory Park, close to the site of Prittlewell Priory, founded in 1110. The priory was a self-contained community of black-robed Cluniac Benedictine monks. Simon and some of his friends were in the park when one of the students, Carolyn, took a photograph of a girl resting on the park bench. When the students looked at the negative, they saw an odd figure standing over the girl. The contact print was sent to Kodak but none of the technicians could discern what the dark shape could be. There were no shrubs near the bench. Sightings of monks were often reported in Priory Park – maybe that day one of them decided to pay a visit?

Ashingdon

St Andrew's church is believed to have been founded by King Canute to commemorate his victory in battle on the hill where the church now stands. Though lawns surround the church today, legend says that after the battle no grass would grow on the bloodstained hill.

Brentwood

The spirit of the young Protestant martyr William Hunter, born in Brentwood in 1536, is said to haunt the old Swan Inn in Brentwood High Street. The return to Roman Catholicism under Queen Mary provoked tremendous protest in Essex. Those who refused to recant their Protestant views were burnt at the stake. At least twenty-three Protestants were burned at Colchester, including six in one fire. Seventeen Essex men and women from Bocking and Stratford were burnt at Smithfield, and other burnings of people from Rayleigh, Braintree, Maldon and Horndon took place.

The nineteen-year-old Hunter, who had been apprenticed to a silk weaver in London, was a fervent Protestant and was dismissed by his employer when he refused to receive communion at the Easter Mass. He was sent home to Brentwood and one day was found in the chapel reading the Bible, which was heresy under Mary's law and punishable by burning.

Although given the chance to recant, Hunter refused and was sentenced to death in his home town. He lodged at the Swan Inn two days prior to his execution and said a poignant goodbye to his parents and friends on the morning of his death. On Tuesday 26 March 1555, he was burned at the stake 'at the town's end, where the butts stood', in the presence of the townspeople, including Sir Antony Browne, the lord of the manor. Tradition assigned the site of Hunter's martyrdom to a great elm tree which stood by Brentwood School for centuries, before its dead trunk was replaced by an oak to mark the accession to the throne of King George VI in 1936. In 1861, the Hunter Memorial was erected in Shenfield Road, paid for by public subscription.

Numerous sightings of William Hunter have been reported over the years at the Swan, which was rebuilt in 1935, although it is believed that the sixteenth-century Swan was across the road. In 1963, the daughter of the then licensee reported that she saw a man wearing an old-fashioned hat follow her mother across the landing one night. Renee McCarthy, another girl, was given a bedroom at the pub but the supernatural activity so alarmed her that she left and refused ever to visit the pub again. Wall-mounted plates have been hurled from shelves onto the floor, bumping sounds have been heard coming from the cellar and furniture has been moved about mysteriously during the night. Lights have inexplicably been switched on and off and doors have locked themselves. Papers have vanished only to be found in another part of the building. A dog kept by one landlord refused to enter certain parts of the building.

Another ancient inn along Brentwood's London Road is the Golden Fleece. Although it has seen much refurbishment, it still retains within its roof many original beams. This building stands on the site of the twelfth-century Priory of St Peter's and is haunted by yet another monk, which has been seen by many people over the last century. This monk is usually reflected in the mirror and stands behind the person with his arms crossed. Poltergeist activity has been reported in the Golden Fleece by young waitresses and bar staff who have mentioned their cooking utensils being moved inexplicably around the kitchen.

Right: William Hunter dying in the flames, 1555.

Below: William Hunter – the old tree stump.

The ghosts of nine navvies haunt the embankment near the Seven Arches Bridge in Brentwood. One foggy night in 1840, soon after the opening of the Eastern Counties Railway line at Brentwood, the men were unloading ballast trucks when they heard a train approaching. They all seemed to think that the oncoming train was on the same line as the train they were unloading, so jumped off. Unfortunately, they were all cut to pieces. Their remains were gathered up and put into the engine shed at Brentwood railway station. After an inquest had been held, the fragments were wrapped in nine squares of calico and put in coffins, then buried on the north side of the parish church.

The Seven Arches Bridge, close to where the nine workers died.

Great Leighs

During the Second World War, Great Leighs, near Chelmsford, was the place that brought the London press reporters to this part of Essex. An unknown woman, suspected of being a witch, had been executed in the seventeenth century and had been buried with a stake through her heart at the nearby crossroads, now known as Scrapfaggot Green. On top of the grave had been placed a huge stone, supposedly preventing the witch from leaving her grave.

In 1944, during the course of road-widening to enable heavy military vehicles to proceed to and from the nearby US Army base, a bulldozer was moved in to remove the boulder from the site. The spirit of the witch is said to have been released. Almost immediately, strange things began happening. The clock on the parish church began chiming backwards and the church bells began pealing by themselves. Cows stopped giving milk and geese disappeared without trace. Hens stopped laying and one farmer found his chickens had mysteriously transferred themselves to his duck pen some distance away. Sceptics suggested that this was the work of a practical joker but at the time many seriously believed that supernatural forces were at work.

The stone was returned to its old resting place at Scrapfaggot Green and life returned to normal in the village. The stone now rests in front of the old St Anne's Castle pub at Great Leighs. This ancient pub has its own set of ghostly characters. They so intrigued its owners that a group of ghost-hunters were invited to spend an all-night vigil in the building. Some interesting 'visitors', who have also been seen on several occasions by the owners and staff, were recorded. An apparition believed to be Anne Hughes, who in 1621 was accused of being a witch and was hanged, is often seen in the old pub, and a black cat, presumably belonging to

Anne, has been seen. Then there was Elizabeth, who walks around the owners' bedroom in her wedding dress, frequently going to the window to stare out. But perhaps the most interesting is the monk who sits in the bar smoking a pipe – a very strong smell of tobacco is frequently wafted through the pub.

Stock

The ghost of Charlie 'Spider' Marshall haunts the Bear Inn at Stock, but this spirit is a somewhat friendly one. Spider was an ostler at the Bear Inn at the end of the nineteenth century. He had no home of his own and no family. He lived in the stables of the inn. He earned his nickname by his peculiar way of walking sideways, like a spider crab. For the amusement of the regulars at the Bear, who would give him a few pence, he would scramble up the chimney of the taproom fireplace and emerge from the chimney in the bar parlour. Occasionally, however, he would stay up the chimney for some time to unnerve the customers and pop down when least expected. The only way to bring him down would be to light a fire in one of the fireplaces to smoke him out. There was a small loft at the junction of the two chimneys where Spider would sit listening to his friends entreating him to come down.

One Christmas Eve, however, Spider refused to come down, even when fires were lit to smoke him out, and he was never seen alive again. It was assumed that he had died of suffocation at the junction of both chimneys but no attempt was made to remove his body and it is presumed that his remains are still there. However, a little man is often to be seen late at night in the bar wearing his white breeches and boots, and every year the locals drink his health at Christmas time.

St Osyth

The remains of this twelfth-century priory have been the scene of nocturnal activity by a ghostly monk, who has been seen carrying a lighted candle around the ruins late at night before meandering down to the millstream, where, after a few seconds, he disappears. Wearing a white robe, he was a regular visitor before the Second World War and has certainly been seen as late as 1970.

Tilty

A headless monk is the ghost connected with the old Cistercian abbey at Tilty. He is to be occasionally seen walking down Cherry Lane. In 1215, King John ravaged Essex and his soldiers broke into the abbey, which was rich and prosperous in its early years. The monks were said to have put up a strong resistance to protect their property. As a result, one monk was beheaded. During the 1940s, some ancient graves by the side of the abbey were excavated. In one of the graves, the skeleton was said to be minus its skull.

Rayleigh

In the mid-1960s, a young girl was riding on the back of her brother's motorbike on the main road from London to Southend. As they were approaching the Rayleigh Weir junction, there was an accident in which the girl was thrown from the bike and killed. The following year, a young lad was having a spin on his motorbike. Approaching the lay-by on the approach at Rayeigh Weir, he saw a girl dressed in motorcycle gear hitching a lift. He picked her up and as they sped along she gave him her name and address. When the lad stopped at the first set of traffic lights, he realised that the girl was no longer on the back of his bike. He travelled back as far as the Weir junction but there was no trace of her. He phoned the police, who sent an officer to the address given by the girl. He was amazed to learn that she could not have been on the Southend road that night because she had been killed at Rayleigh a year previously.

Weeley

Stately homes and manor houses can usually boast a ghost or two, perhaps an aristocratic lady or a knight with a suitably historic pedigree. But others find that their particular apparition may come from below stairs, and rather than drifting aimlessly along the battlements or causing cold draughts in the great hall, ghostly servants have sometimes been known to make themselves useful. The Manor House at Weeley has long enjoyed the services of a very helpful ghost. One past resident was surprised and pleased to find that while he was out, his room had been mysteriously tidied up. Even more amazingly, a complete dinner service was once moved from the kitchen dresser, cleaned and returned. Not content with this, the ghostly housekeeper had given the whole kitchen a good spring clean.

Colchester

The Essex County Hospital at Colchester seems an unlikely place for a ghost story, especially in the children's ward, but a local man has never forgotten what happened when he was a patient there as a child. He was in bed one night when he saw a nun in a black habit coming towards him. She spoke kindly to him and give him a toffee from a brown paper bag she was carrying. Surprised, he popped it in his mouth and watched as she walked on down the ward and couldn't believe it when she then just disappeared in front of his eyes.

Danbury

Betty Puttick, Essex ghost-hunter extraordinaire, visited Danbury church a few years ago and came across the intriguing tale of a visitation by the Devil. On Corpus Christi Day in 1402, during evensong, there was a violent storm which broke part of the steeple and damaged the chancel. At the height of the tempest, the Devil himself was seen 'in the likeness of a Friar Minor, who entering the church, raged insolently to the great terror of the parishioners … the top of the steeple was broken down and half the chancel scattered abroad'.

Theydon Mount

Sir Thomas Smith, an eminent nobleman during Queen Mary's reign, managed to lead a quiet life during the religious ferment of the late Tudor reign. He rebuilt Hill House, the lovely manor house at Theydon Mount, Epping. Among the owners who followed him was a family with a beautiful daughter. Seven brothers courted her but she could not make up her mind and suggested that they fight a seven-cornered duel for her hand. The girl watched every one of the brothers fight to their death. It was said that bloodstains marked the walls and door of the room where they died. The remorseful girl, dressed in bridal finery, committed suicide and every so often her ghost appears in the grounds of Hill House. The house is now in the care of English Heritage.

Little Baddow

Little Baddow near Chelmsford is believed to be haunted by the Devil. Set in the north wall of Little Baddow's fourteenth-century church is an unadorned entrance known as a Devil Door. To medieval Christians, the north side of the church was the province of Satan. It was on the left-hand side facing the altar and Christ had said that he would set 'the sheep on His right hand and the goats on His left'. Because of this, baptisms were performed in the south porch of the church. If an infant cried after being christened, it was traditionally thought to be a sign that the Devil had been driven from its soul and the north door, which was left open during the ceremony, allowed Satan to escape 'to his own place'.

Billericay

The old Billericay Union Workhouse in Norsey Road was built in 1840 and served twenty-six surrounding parishes. In 1898, St Andrew's Hospital was built and the orchards and gardens of the old workhouse were used to build wards and an extension. Both patients and nurses reported seeing a small lady dressed in grey walk through the wards during late evening. When the hospital was demolished to make way for a new housing complex on the site, one of the roads was called Grey Lady Place.

Another haunted place is not far away in Billericay High Street, where Burghstead Lodge, a lovely Georgian building, stands. Several ghosts have been reported here and a woman dressed in a long green gown is supposed to haunt the second floor. In her book *Yesterday – A Childhood in Billericay*, Edith Sparvel-Bayly states that while she lived in the Lodge as a child, she and her two sisters often saw a white lady wandering the shrubbery bordering Brentwood Road. The police station now stands on the site.

Maldon

The legendary Black Shuck once roamed the villages around Maldon. The word 'shuck' is said to derive from the old English *scocca*, which translates as 'demonic' and 'terror'. This hellish hound, in the form of a huge black dog with fiery red eyes, was reported to have been seen as he roamed the coastline of Maldon. He is said to have sailed with the Vikings to our coast in AD 991, in one of the most famous invasions of our coastline – the Battle of Maldon, where Byrhtnoth was defeated and killed.

Burghstead Lodge, which is haunted by two women.

EIGHT

TELLING TALES

Tell me the old, old story.
Kate Hankey (1834-1911)

Everyone loves a tale and this is the natural way that much folklore has been passed down through the generations. With the advent of television and all the high-tech communication that surrounds us, the art of storytelling seemed in danger of being lost. Happily, Jan Williams of Brightlingsea founded the Essex Storytellers in the early 1990s. The group then comprised of Jan, the late Peter Maskens and Carl Merry. Andy Jennings joined them in 2004. They have successfully revived a collection of carefully researched stories from Essex and they enjoy telling the tales at festivals, schools, theatres, libraries and folk clubs, not only in the county but throughout East Anglia.

The Essex Storytellers. From left to right: Carl Merry, Jan Williams, Andy Jennings.

Mersea Island is the setting for one tale from the Essex Storytellers. The island lies between the Colne and Blackwater rivers and is linked to Colchester by a causeway known as the Strood. A Roman burial mound lies unnoticed on the road to East Mersea, its original height decreased through time and erosion. However, for those aware of its existence, it has provoked romantic but ghostly tales.

The Mersea barrow was excavated in May 1912 by the notable archaeologist Samuel Hazzledine Warren (1872-1958). He considered the barrow had been built between AD 60 and 96 for a person of great importance, maybe a local ruler. A 12ft-wide central shaft was built, connecting with a short passageway. At first, disappointingly, it exposed nothing but fragments of pottery, flints and oyster shells, then, after a month, a tomb was revealed containing a beautiful green glass burial urn in a lead box. Amazingly, this Roman urn, which was removed from the tomb, transported to Colchester Castle by car and taken from its tight-fitting casket, was found to be without a single scratch. It is impossible to tell if the cremated bones within were those of a man or a woman. After the excavation, the shaft and tunnel were filled in and a tunnel dug to make it possible for visitors to see the tomb chamber at the barrow's heart. Hazzledine Warren came to the curious conclusion that there was a ghost but 'not a ghost possessing any notable or distinctive personality'. The Essex Storytellers know better.

Nonsense Tales

People moving to the town of Coggeshall are intrigued when they hear the term 'Coggeshall jobs' – the famous nonsense tales from the past. Local folk obviously have a great sense of humour and rarely take offence at the inferred stupidity. Alison Barnes, in her book *Coggeshall Jobs*, describes thirty such tales, which poke harmless fun at the fictitious antics of the villagers trying to fish the moon out of the river Blackwater, thinking it was a ball of gold; putting their clocks forward to make summer come round more quickly; placing a rope across a meadow to stop the spreading of a flood; or shutting the turnpike gate to keep out smallpox. Unlike fables, Coggeshall jobs have no real moral and their chief purpose is simply to amuse – which they do!

The element of fantasy contained in the tales stimulates the imagination and opens up unusual new vistas to the mind. In the early 1600s, many classic 'noodle' jokes appeared in English jest books and spread widely throughout the country. Noodle tales are related in England to the Men of Gotham in Nottinghamshire and the Carles of Austwick in Yorkshire, but similar tales can be found in the folklore of countries all over the world.

The Essex Calf

The term 'Essex calf', which seems to have originated in medieval times and is referred to in Aphra Behn's Restoration plays, refers to the tale of an Essex farmer's prize calf. One day, it jammed its head between the bars of a five-barred gate. Up rushed the locals, who stood scratching their heads, trying to work out a way of releasing the poor trapped animal. One bright lad, a little more astute than the others, thought of a way and soon the calf was free – he had struck off its head with an axe. Hence the nickname 'Essex calf', which was once well known.

However, our Essex calves were perhaps not as foolish as they seemed. A plain country fellow born in Essex, coming to London for the first time, was intrigued by the bell-pull with its bright shiny handle that hung outside the door of a merchant's house. Never having seen such a thing, he wondered what it was and, taking it up in his hand to examine it, he accidentally rang the bell. The merchant, a somewhat pompous man, came to the door and asked him what he wanted. 'Nothing, sir,' said he. 'I was just looking at this pretty gadget that hangs at your door.' 'What countryman are you?' asked the merchant. 'An Essex man,' replied the other. 'I thought so,' said the merchant, 'for I have heard say that if a man beat a bush in Essex, there presently comes forth a calf.' 'It may be so,' rejoined the countryman, 'and I think a man can no sooner ring a bell in London, but out pops a donkey!'

AN ESSEX LEGEND

| Years ago a foolish calf
Through a fast-closed gate
Tightly fixed his thick-set head,
And met a sorry fate. | For a crowd of villagers
Rushed to set him free ;
Alas, the way they did it
Was by beheading he. | Now Essex men and maidens,
This may be true or not,
For the nickname " Essex calves "
Is almost now forgot. |

A 1906 postcard telling the tale of the Essex calf.

Thomasine Tyler

Great changes occurred in the growing hamlet of Brentwood following the Reformation. Much of the land in the area had been held by the Church. When the monasteries were dissolved, the manor of South Weald came under the jurisdiction of Sir Antony Browne, who lived at Weald Hall. Following his death, his great-nephew, Wistan Browne, inherited the estate.

Ten years later, Wistan decided to stop paying the chaplain and close the chapel. The people of Brentwood became angry and a petition was sent to the Lord Keeper of the Great Seal, complaining that the new lord had closed their chapel. With an armed guard, he had removed the pulpit, pews, church bell and clock. Parishioners also complained that they were now forced to travel long distances to South Weald to attend church.

Wistan should have realised the strength of feeling of the townsfolk, who loved their chapel in which local folk had worshipped for 300 years. It was all too much for Thomasine Tyler, wife of a property owner in the town. One day in August 1577, she and twenty-nine other angry women marched down the High Street. They were armed with 'pitchforks, bills, a piked staff, two hot spits, three bows, nine arrows, one hatchet, one great hammer, hot water in two kettles and a great sharp stone'. The furious women pulled schoolmaster Richard Brooke from the chapel, beat him and barricaded themselves inside.

Eventually, Wistan and his men were able to arrest Thomasine and the other women, carting them off to prison, and the protest ended suddenly and ingloriously for the brave women. Wistan Browne was ordered to appear before the powerful privy council and told to refrain from pulling down the chapel. He was also ordered to release the women from prison on bail. The women were fined fourpence and Wistan was forced to restore the chapel to Brentwood.

Anne Boleyn's Head

From the time that Henry VIII's second wife, Anne Boleyn, was executed on 19 May 1536, after just 1,000 days as Queen of England, there has been conjecture as to the whereabouts of her head. Arthur Mee, in his book *Essex*, first published in 1940, suggests that Anne's head was taken to East Horndon church, on the southern edge of Thorndon Park, not far from Brentwood. Standing high upon a windswept hill, this ancient church is associated with generations of the Tyrell family, whose ancestor Ralph Tyrell is believed to have slain William Rufus in the New Forest in 1100. Historians have long thought that Anne's body had been dumped in an old chest used for storing arrows and buried in the grounds of St Peter's church at the Tower of London.

Essex historian Norman Gunby feels that Anne's sister Mary – who had retired to Rochford Hall, the childhood home of the Boleyn family – retrieved Anne's head from the executioner in an attempt to take it to Rochford, to prevent the indignity of it being stuck on the end of a pike on London Bridge. During repairs to East Horndon church in 1876, a skeleton was discovered which, according to examining experts, was of young woman. Anne Boleyn was just twenty-nine at her execution but if the skeleton had been hers, there could have been no mistaking it, as Anne was born with six fingers on each hand. Yet another Essex village, Horndon-on-the-Hill, lays claim to being the resting place of the unfortunate queen.

Essex Serpents

For centuries, dragons have been a recurring favourite theme for the storyteller. Although they are supposedly mythical creatures, they are mentioned in the Bible and Shakespeare often included them in his plays. On St George's Day, the cartoonists have a field day sketching variations of flame-snorting monsters being slain by England's patron saint.

Essex appears to have gained something of a reputation for attracting exotic creatures of this nature. Herbert Tompkins, in his book *Companion Into Essex*, told his readers about a flying serpent that one day appeared in the village of Henham. He tracked down a pamphlet, dated 1669, which was written by Peter Lillycrap, owner of a printing press in Clerkenwell Close. The title page is intriguing in itself, declaring:

> The flying serpent or strange news out of Essex, being a true relation of a monstrous serpent which hath diverse times been seen at a parish called Henham-on-the mount within four miles of Saffron Walden, showing the length, proportion, the bigness of the serpent, the place where it commonly lurks and what means hath been used to kill it.

This was prefaced by enigmatic homily that 'guests, fish and news grow stale in three days' time'. The Henham creature was 'eight or nine feet long, the smallest part of him about the bigness of a man's leg, or the middle as big as a man's thigh'. It was apparently seen on 27 May 1669 by several Henham villagers, including the churchwarden, the constable and John Knight, overseer of the poor. The fearsome creature had large, piercing eyes, two rows of very white, very sharp teeth and two wings 'about two handfuls long', which were not strong enough to make him airborne. The pamphlet ended with a postscript that the neighbours intended to keep a constant watch upon it. The serpent disappeared thereafter and was not seen again until the Second World War, when, cashing in on their history, stallholders at the Henham Fair sold miniature dragons and a local brew called Snakebite.

Another tale collected by the late Peter Laurie and included in his book *The Great Serpent of East Horndon* tells of an 'imported' creature that seems to have escaped from a ship in medieval times and made its way through the boggy marshes to East Horndon, finding a home among the tombs of the local churchyard. It came out at night and terrorised the villagers, whom it attacked and devoured. Sir James Tyrell, who owned the local manor of Heron, was a brave and wise man. The parishioners of East Horndon approached Sir James for help. Realising that the creature was more powerful than him, Tyrell knew great cunning was needed to conquer it. Everyone knows that serpents are vain, so the noble knight strapped a looking-glass to his chest. When he approached the serpent, the creature prepared his attack him but paused first to admire his reflection, whereupon Sir James seized his opportunity and killed the monster, bringing the creature's head home to his wife as a gift.

Saffron Walden in the seventeenth century saw yet another, much smaller, serpent or cockatrice, which had been annoying the villagers. Described as being only 1ft long but with red eyes and a sharp head, its flaming breath could kill anything in its path. No plant could grow where it lived and the rumour was that it had killed many townspeople. Again, to the rescue came a knight wearing a 'coat of crystal glass' which reflected the creature's image. Apparently, the purity of the crystal was so repugnant to the nasty little cockatrice that it curled up and died. The knight became a hero and his sword was hung in the church, where a brass effigy of the cockatrice was also placed.

Story of a Bridge

An interesting folktale from Stratford, once part of Essex, concerns Bow Bridge. Stratford stands at the boundary of London and Essex, straddling the Roman road to Colchester. Its name comes from the Roman street that fords the Lea, and its location at the river's shallowest crossing made Stratford a convenient gateway from London into Essex. The ford there had existed since Saxon times. Local legend tells us that one day when Matilda Maud – who was also Abbess of Barking at the time and wife of Henry I – was crossing the Lea at Old Ford, she slipped and got her feet wet. As a consequence, she persuaded Henry I to build a bridge over the Lea.

The construction of the bridge marked an important step in communications. Although there had been bridges across streams since early times, this was the first stone-arched bridge in England. Earlier bridges had been simply timber planks thrown across at narrow points. Even the famous London Bridge, mention of which dates back to Saxon times, had been entirely constructed of timber. The bridge consisted of seven stone arches sweeping across the river in a gentle bow; this is the probable explanation for the name it has borne ever since – Bow Bridge. It stood for 700 years under the care of two parishes, one half in Essex and the other in Middlesex. By 1827, only three of the seven arches were visible, the others being incorporated in the cellars of houses that had been built on it. In 1835, a single-span bridge in granite replaced it, but by 1905 even this graceful successor proved inadequate and it was pulled down and replaced by the iron bridge we see today.

The Great Edward Bright

Maldon claims the fattest man in eighteenth-century Essex. This was Edward Bright, who, when he died in 1750 at the age of twenty-nine, weighed 44 stones. Bright was once a post boy and rode regularly to Chelmsford and back. He lived at the Church House near St Peter's in the High Street, where he later kept a shop. When he died, a hole had to be cut into the wall of his house and an improvised crane employed to lower his coffin. Six strong men carried him out of the front gate and placed him on the hearse. He was buried at All Saints church, Maldon.

Following Bright's death, a wager was made between Mr Hance and Mr Codd of Maldon. Was it possible to fit 700 men inside the waistcoat of their recently deceased friend? The answer was yes, as the person proposing the bet had meant 'seven Hundred men', i.e. seven men from Dengie Hundred (the district in which Maldon lay).

Edward Bright Junior, also a sturdy lad but never more than half his father's weight, left nine children and the name of Bright is still a great one in Maldon, but thankfully none of his descendants have been of extraordinary size.

Edward Bright of Maldon.

Essex Marsh Wives

In his *A Tour Through Great Britain*, published in 1724, Daniel Defoe had much to say about the marshlands of Essex:

> I have one remark more before I leave this damp part of the world, and which I cannot omit on the women's account: namely, that I took notice of a strange decay of the sex here; inasmuch, that all along this county it was very frequent to meet with men that had had from five or six to fourteen or fifteen wives; nay, and some more; and I was inform'd that in the marshes on the other side of the river over against Candy Island, there was a farmer, who was then living with the five and twentieth wife, and that his son who was but about thirty-five years old, had already had about fourteen; indeed this part of the story I only had by report, tho' from good hands too; but the other is well known and easie to be inquired into, about Fobbing, Corringham, Thundersley, Benfleet, Prittlewell, Wakering, Great Stambridge, Cricksea, Burnham, Dengy and other towns of the like situation.
>
> The reason as a merry fellow told me, who said he had had about a dozen and a half of wives (tho' I found out afterwards he fibbed a little) was this: That they being bred in the marshes themselves, and season'd to the place, did pretty well with it; but that they always went up into the hilly country, or, to speak their own language, into the uplands for a wife. That when they took the young lasses out of the wholesome and fresh air, they were healthy, fresh and clear and well; but when they came out of their native air into the marshes among the fogs and damps, there they presently chang'd their complexion, got an ague or two, and seldom held it above half a year, or a year at most; and then, said he, we go to the uplands again and fetch another; so that marrying of wives was reckon'd a kind of good farm to them. It is true, the fellow told this in a kind of drollery, and mirth; but the fact, for all that, is certainly true; and that they have abundance of wives by that very means.

Smuggling Days

The wild days of smuggling in the Essex marshes are kept alive by old legends and chance discoveries. When the Peter Boat Inn at Leigh-on-Sea was reconstructed a century ago, a warren of secret storage cellars was discovered beneath the building. In Manningtree at one time, all the upper lofts in the village were linked together so that smugglers could make their escape. In the days when smuggling was a profitable business, the Colne, Blackwater and Crouch, and the north bank of the Thames, with their numerous tributaries, all protected by sea walls, gave every facility and protection for running cargoes.

Smuggling was widespread for centuries, although there is a general impression that it only started in Napoleon's day. Dr Samuel Johnson, famous for the dictionary he compiled, which was first published in 1755, defined a smuggler as 'a wretch who, in defiance of justice and the laws, imports or export goods without contraband or without payment of the customs'. And yet Johnson had no compunction in being 'a hardened and shameless tea drinker ... whose kettle has scarcely time to cool'. It was very probable that his housekeeper may have known of a smuggler's agent who could get his tea a little cheaper.

There is clear evidence of smuggling in Essex more than 600 years ago, to evade the tax on the export of wool. The tax was imposed during the reign of Edward I and it was he who introduced the impressive King's Beams, huge scales for weighing the wool which were set up at every Custom House in the country. The address of the headquarters of HM Customs & Excise is still shown as King's Beam House in the City of London.

The illegal export of wool reached such huge proportions that, in 1698, 300 Riding Officers were appointed by the Government to patrol, on horseback, the long coastal areas. Each one was responsible for a 10-mile stretch. It was an impossible task. The intention was to deter and catch the smugglers landing contraband along the lonely and isolated coastline. By 1713, the Riding Officers were receiving support from garrisons of troops encamped at strategic points from which they could quickly give assistance to any place along the Essex coast. They were fighting a losing battle and some also lost their lives in the process.

The Essex coastline was ideal for smuggling. Low-lying, bleak and lonely, it made a perfect landfall for a swift ship loaded with a cargo of contraband. The Revenue Service was poorly staffed and financed and its cutters were easily eluded by local seamen, who knew how to pick their way through the maze of tidal creeks and channels in the broad estuaries.

During its heyday, smuggling embraced a huge range of luxuries on which a duty should have been paid, including lace, silks, coffee and playing cards, as well as less orthodox cargo such as golden guineas. It was huge industry, employing thousands of people, and was said to account for a quarter of all England's overseas trade. The sea walls hid the land operations of the smugglers from the revenue cutter patrolling the rivers or possibly chasing a smuggling craft, while the Riding Officer on the land could see nothing of what was happening on the water unless he was actually on the wall or on the waterside. There was reluctance to take such a vantage point as the officer would be a good target.

Whole communities were involved in this black economy – young and old, rich and poor, labourers and landowners. Along the Essex coast, it was not uncommon to see 100 carts and as many horses gathered on the beach to await a large landing of contraband, which was soon efficiently spirited away for distribution to the waiting markets of Colchester, Chelmsford and London. Country gentlemen, farmers and even parsons were all more or less in league with the smugglers, and those that did not take a physical part in the proceedings turned a blind eye. No marshland farmer worried when he found his horse had been borrowed during the night, as he knew that he would find a keg or two lurking in his stable in the morning.

At Hadleigh Castle, phantoms known as the White Lady and the Black Man often made dramatic appearances but oddly enough only before the arrival of a shipment of illicit liquor. The castle's gaunt ruins, which still look out grimly over Hadleigh Bay, Canvey and Leigh, were said to have been a favourite hiding place, while several churches are also credited with having been storage places for smuggled wares. Rochford church and Canvey church were sometimes used as hiding places for contraband, the latter being particularly convenient when there had been a run via Hole Haven, across the island to the mainland. Around 1800, it was said that the entire population of Paglesham was engaged in this 'free trade'. In one year, they smuggled in more than 13,000 gallons of Geneva (gin) and brandy and £200 worth of silk at a time was hidden in the hollow elms at East Hall.

Tales of ghostly spectres were cleverly exploited by local smugglers to cloak their operations. Tiptree Heath was a favourite place used as a distribution area, while a favourite landing place for contraband was Brandy Hole Creek on the Crouch. From there, tubs of brandy were conveyed in shrimp carts across Daws Heath, near Rayleigh, to their final destination in London. Brandy smugglers working along the Crouch would use a 'ghost cart' – a cart washed with luminous paint and with muffled wheels – to frighten unwanted visitors away.

The lonely creeks witnessed bloody and desperate fights, with no mercy on either side. A whole boatload of Excise men with their throats cut was found on Sunken Island near Mersea in the early 1800s. They now lie buried beneath their upturned boat in Virley churchyard.

Hadleigh Castle ruins.

Three Wives in Seven Weeks

Quoted in *The Chelmsford and Colchester Chronicle* on 21 October 1768 was the story of the farmer at Halstead who buried a wife on 1 September and married a second on 8 September. She died on 4 October and he 'took a third partner to his arms on Wednesday last'.

The Bigamist of Thorpe-le-Soken

In the *Evening Post* of 15 August 1752, a story was published concerning a gentleman who had disembarked on the Colne river with a large box which, when opened, was seen to contain the embalmed body of a beautiful young women. After interrogation, he was allowed to travel to Thorpe-le-Soken with his strange burden and called upon the Revd Alexander Gough, the vicar of the parish. He asked him to fulfil the last wish of the dead woman, which was that she should be buried in the churchyard there.

The vicar was surprised but was infinitely astonished when he recognised the lifeless face of his own wife, who had deserted him three years earlier. The gentleman declared himself to be Lord Dalmeny, eldest son of Lord Rosebery, who had been born in Italy and had met and married Catherine Canham in Verona. On her deathbed, Catherine had confessed her bigamy. She desperately wanted to be buried back in the churchyard at Thorpe. With her two husbands accompanying the casket, no stranger funeral had ever been witnessed at Thorpe-le-Soken.

A Farmer's Funeral

From the *Lincoln Mercury* of 18 February 1785:

> A few days since died at Upper Yeldham Hall in Essex, Mr Hurrell farmer and maltster, aged 95. He ordered in his will that his body should be interred in one of his woods, be covered with one of his hair cloths he used to dry his malt on; and that six hedgers and ditchers should carry his corpse, six others be pall bearers and six more follow as mourners, all with their bills and hedging gloves; and likewise ordered a hogshead of old beer to be drunk.

The Georgian Age

In September 1714, young Richard Barrett wrote home to his father at Belhus, Aveley, describing how he had watched the ship bearing the first of the Georges pass between Tilbury and Gravesend and had then gone to Greenwich, where the

King landed at dusk by torchlight. Later that night, he was presented to the King and the Prince of Wales. He had witnessed the beginning of the Georgian Age.

Fiddler Dring

The coming of the railway to Essex brought prosperity to the Great Eastern Railway directors but put many of the coaches, carriers and carters out of business. For fifty years, Fiddler Dring, the coachman of the *Yarmouth Star*, had made the journey from London to Norwich, sleeping in the City of London one night and Norwich the next. On the morning of his last journey in 1843, while driving his coach down Crown Street to the railway station, the coach wheels ran on to the fence of the field, making 'such a clatter on the fence' that it frightened the four horses and they bolted. In turning the corner down the first hill, where it joins Queen's Road, over went the coach, the driver and all the passengers into the field. Strange to say, no one was hurt, except poor old Fiddler Dring, who was killed on the spot.

Essex Divinations

Marriage was considered the most important event of a girl's life in times past. Across the county, the snail, known locally as hodmedod or dodman, was often called on by superstitious girls when they wanted to learn about their future husbands. Anxious to discover the initials of her true love, a girl placed a poor old snail on a saucer or piece of slate and left it overnight. By morning, the initials of the gentleman would be there in a trail of slime.

There were many other rituals used by lovelorn maidens to discover who their future spouse might be. The well-known chants 'He loves me, he loves me not' and 'Tinker, tailor, soldier, sailor' when counting cherry or prune stones or plucking petals from a daisy are familiar even today. In Colchester at the beginning of the last century, Kathleen Curtis's sisters would peel a cooking apple so that the skin stayed in one piece, stand on a chair and drop the skin to the floor. In this way, they might determine the initial of their new love.

From Saffron Walden, the superstition concerning ladybirds is also well known. On finding a ladybird, a girl would place it on the back of her hand and gently blow it away after reciting the rhyme:

> Bishy, bishy Barnabee
> Tell me when my wedding will be,
> If it be tomorrow day,
> Take your wings and fly away,
> Fly to the East, fly to the West
> Fly to him I love the best.

A Pirate in Essex

A tale that has entered the realms of modern folklore is that of Radio Caroline, the first pirate radio station to broadcast pop music from an old Dutch coaster, the *Mi Amigo*, anchored off the Essex coast. The station, which illegally operated without a broadcasting licence, was named after the late President Kennedy's daughter, Caroline, and was an immediate success with young people. It was an important part of the 'swinging sixties'.

On 19 January 1966, a vicious snow-laden wind hit the *Mi Amigo* so hard that it broke from its moorings and blew ashore at Great Holland. The Walton lifeboatmen had enormous difficulties in launching a rescue attempt. At last, the pirate had been silenced, but not for long. The *Mi Amigo* was repaired and Radio Caroline was back in action just 13 miles off the Essex coast at Southend – just outside UK territorial waters. On 20 March 1980, Radio Caroline again met storms that blew the ship, anchor and equipment off its mooring and into the graveyard of so many boats. The Sheerness lifeboat rescuers pulled the four men to safety and the *Mi Amigo* sank into the sands. Where the Government had failed, the elements succeeded. By 1983, Caroline was back on air transmitting from the *Revenge*, a converted trawler in the harsh waters of the North Sea. In all, Radio Caroline had been in and out of the news for more than twenty-five years.

A Pearly Tale

Benfleet is the home of Mr and Mrs Christopher Friend, who continue the Pearly King and Queen tradition in Essex, raising money for many charities. The custom started in London in 1875. That year, thirteen-year-old Henry Croft left his orphanage to seek work, finding a job as a roadsweeper and ratcatcher in Somers Town market, St Pancras. The lad enjoyed the company of the costermongers, who sold fruit and vegetables, and was intrigued with the way the 'costers' sewed a row of pearl buttons along their trouser seams. He also loved their friendliness and the way they helped each other in times of sickness. Henry collected mother-of-pearl buttons from the 'sweat shops' around the market and sewed them on to his jacket, continuing until his entire suit was covered. This started the tradition. The Pearly Kings create intricate designs and sew on thousands of buttons, sometimes as many as 40,000, making their clothes very heavy.

Henry's charitable work began in hospitals and workhouses. His costermonger friends helped and became the first Pearly families. When he died in 1930, he had raised over £5,000, approximately £½ million pounds in today's money. His funeral was a spectacular affair, filmed by Pathe News. More than 400 Pearlies followed his coffin. Henry's descendants still carry on the Pearly tradition and there are several other Pearlies in Essex towns.

Mr and Mrs Christopher Friend, Pearly King and Queen living in Benfleet.

Emergency Call

The free 999 telephone emergency system was introduced in May 1928 because of serious delays in police response following the murder of one of their constables in Essex. Alec Ward, a mail van driver, was first on the scene of the brutal murder of PC George Gutteridge on 27 September 1927 on the lonely Stapleford Abbots road. The policeman had been shot four times in the head, including a bullet through each eye. Desperately needing police help, Ward drove immediately to Stapleford Tawney post office and tried to ring the Romford police station but his call was refused, as they said that PC Gutteridge was not stationed there. They suggested Ward should ring Ongar police. When the telephone operator demanded payment for the call, the postmistress had to intervene in the ensuing argument. So much time had elapsed following the discovery of the policeman's body that the hunt for the murderers was seriously delayed. Eventually, the killers, Frederick Browne and William Kennedy, were arrested, convicted at the Old Bailey and hanged in 1928. It seems that they shot the policeman through each eye as they believed the superstition that the eye of a dead person reflects the image of the last person seen.

As a result, the following notice appeared in the *Daily Mail* on 8 May 1928:

> Notices that fire, police and ambulance emergency calls may be made free are being affixed to public telephone call boxes in London. Later they will be put up throughout the country. Telephone operators have now received strict instructions to put through without delay all such calls. In the Automatic telephone boxes the twopence used to secure a reply from the exchange will be returned after the call has been made.

Nine

County Sounds

The voice she do change in time...
Anon

As the old rural world of Essex passed away, many traditions also disappeared, along with the dialect, songs and, in some cases, place names, although some show an amazing capacity for survival.

In the past, language, speech patterns and the old songs and rhymes of Essex were important when it came to passing on history and folklore by word of mouth, long before they were committed to paper. A good memory was essential for repeating family history, customs and stories from the past. Before the 1870 Education Act, which made education for children compulsory, many country folk could neither read nor write. In a sense, dialect is as much a part of the body of folklore as the way in which it was told. Writer Richard Thomas, in his book *Larn Yarsel Essex Dialect* (1999), suggested that:

> 'Learn' and 'learning' are used generally in Essex for 'teach' and 'teaching'. In addition, learning means education. The word 'learn' goes back to the Old English *lieran* which means teach and it is interesting to note that, in modern German, lehren means to teach. So an Essex father might say to his son, 'I'll larn you how ter do that boy.' This might be to help him or to punish him for a wrongdoing. Whichever is the case, it takes the use of learn in Essex right back to its Germanic roots.

These days, the wide variety in vernacular speech from East Anglia to Cockney – from the seaboard at Harwich to more Home Counties accents on the Hertfordshire border – is only matched by our hugely varying landscape. It's an interesting journey trying to trace local language through generations of use (and the present misuse), despite the efforts of Victorian and Edwardian England to standardise the spoken word. Essex, bordering London, managed to hang on to its own inimitable dialect into the twentieth century. But with the rapid expansion in population in Essex villages and towns over the last fifty years, things have changed irrevocably.

In 1920, author Edward Gepp, fearful that the Essex dialect and language were disintegrating, compiled a county dictionary in which he interviewed many respondents, recording their words and sayings. To his way of thinking, the changes that were taking place were as a result of the First World War, the movement around the country due to railways and alterations within the educational system. Another Essex writer and historian, Herbert Cranmer-Byng, well-known for his essays and lectures on the subject of 'County Dialect and Humour', reported in 1928: 'Local language is a living culture – dialect is spoken, rarely written, so recording oral history in print has to rely very largely on phonetic spelling and people's memory.'

During the late 1920s and early 1930s, Dagenham, that once tiny ancient village close to the marshes, became the largest council estate in the world. Many of its new residents came from London's suburbs and these 'furriners' brought with them their London and other regional accents, vocabulary, pronunciation, grammar and speech patterns, as well as their slang words, which soon became part of normal use.

Just after the Second World War, there was a huge exodus of people from mainly East London, not only towards Dagenham and Barking but, with excellent rail links, to Chelmsford, Southend and Colchester. Many of these places, including Basildon and Harlow, had been small villages for centuries, until the architects and planners settled at their drawing boards and designed the New Towns, producing yet more 'incomers'.

General movement of people around the county and mass media, especially television, have crowded out our old ways and many now rely on the 'box' as a source of communication and conversation rather than witnessing the events occurring in everyday life. Television programmes such as *Grange Hill* and, more recently, *Eastenders* and *Family Affairs* have influenced the way people, mainly youngsters, speak. It is odd to read press reports that Liverpudlians, Glaswegians and folk from South Wales are beginning to sound like Londoners, using what is now called Estuary English, i.e. dropping consonants and flattening out vowels.

Steve Crancher, in his book *Dijja Wanna Say Sumfing?*, tells us that linguists have been discussing Estuary English since – and probably even before – the term was coined in 1984 by David Rosewarne. At the time, Rosewarne was involved in linguistic research at London's Birkbeck College and his article in the *Times Education Supplement* described the accent/dialect as 'a variety of modified regional speech'. Crancher writes:

> It is generally considered that Estuary English is somewhere on a continuum between Received Pronunciation (BBC or Queen's English) and Cockney. However, while the Hooray Henrys (the young upper class) of the 1980s have long since adopted it in an effort to gain some street credibility, the majority of people

think of Estuary English as that used by Essex Man and Essex Woman (from towns in the south of the county) – that is, the part of the continuum closer to Cockney, than to Received Pronunciation. This is, perhaps, real Estuary English.

Along with the problem of Estuary English, Essex has had a bad press when it comes to county identity. Back in 1988, a tabloid journalist created a fictional stereotyped profile of a typical Essex man and his partner, Essex girl, from which many derogatory books and tabloid column inches have been published and which seem impossible to shake off. Although once humorous, they seem an unfair reflection on the county as a whole and many leading educationalists and Essex county councillors dislike the term. Among the 1½ million residents currently living in the county, probably now only a tiny minority speak in the once true Essex dialect – and these are usually older people living in the northern part of the county.

Old spoken Essex was a true dialect in its own right, not dissimilar to the speech patterns heard in its neighbouring county, Suffolk. James Wentworth Day, writer, raconteur and master of the East Anglian dialect, often included folktales in the county vernacular within his numerous books. In his 1979 *Book of Essex*, he writes:

They were fun, our little country railways. The last breath of rural Victoriana. The authentic puff-puffs of childhood. The pride of the villages ... There was that immortal tale of the opening of the great Eastern Railway in granddad's time. Somewhere along the line there is a tunnel and when the line was opened in the tranquil days of the last century, Jimma bor and Billa bor discussed the momentous event in the inn that night.

'Ha' you sin that li'l owd railrood, Jimma bor?'

'Noo, thet Ah hee'ant. Ha' yu?'

'Yis, bor. Thet run roight at the bottom o' my master's tharty acre. Sharp as yar owd clock goo ten in the mornin'. An' du that travel! Thear ain't a hoss in the parish what could ketch it – nor yit a long-dog. Do yu goo ond see that, Jimma bor.'

'That oi will, oewd mate.'

Sharp at ten the next morning, Jimma bor, his missus and the kids sat like a row of rooks on the five-barred gate above the railway tunnel. On the stroke of the hour the train trundled by in a blast of steam and sparks, gave a piercing whistle and plunged into the dark tunnel, a dragon's tail of sulphuric smoke waving behind it. That night in the four-ale bar came the sequel.

'Ded you see that li'l owd railroad, Jimma bor?'

'See ut! That oi did. Travel, bor! Oi niver seed nawthin' travel that fast in arl moi days. There warn't a hoss at Newmarket what could ha' ketched it. That come a-roarin' an' a-hissin' an' a-flamin' up the valley loike the Davvle hisself. But blast, bor! That ain't that that travel so fast. That ain't that that make so much row. Thass a double-cunnin b--, that is! That no sooner sets that's eyes on me an' the missus an' the kids than that shruk like a hullet [owl] an' hopped down a hole like a rabbit!'

Broadsides and Chapbooks

> And certaynly our language now used varyeth ferre from that which was used and spoken when I was born.
>
> William Caxton (1422-1491)

Although books were being printed in the fifteenth century, only the wealthiest in society could afford to buy them. Most were beyond the reach of ordinary working-class people, who rarely had the leisure time to study them, even if they could read. Many were semi-literate. For over two centuries, from the seventeenth century to the nineteenth century, street literature in the form of chapbooks and broadside ballads provided the basic reading matter of the poor. Chapbooks (or cheap books) were paper-covered booklets, usually of eight to twenty-four pages. The broadside ballads were printed as a single sheet of paper, folio size, and then later a narrow strip on quarto. Both chapbooks and broadside ballads were cheaply produced and poorly printed, often illustrated with crude woodcuts, but they were sold in their hundreds of thousands by specialist printers who, in the earliest days, ran their businesses from properties in London's Seven Dials area.

The content of the chapbooks was varied: ballads, romances, folk tales, jokes, riddles, superstitions, news both true and fabricated, reports of trials, grisly murders, last dying speeches of condemned criminals, amazing wonders, sermons and whatever else the printers and hawkers thought would take the public's fancy. Chapbooks provided the first real children's literature and they proved an excellent means by which folklore could be distributed across Essex.

With the growth of the printing trade, some kind of control had to be introduced before the presses became too powerful. The Stationers' Company, which was founded on 4 May 1557, became the official authority responsible for its members throughout the country, controlling the printing and sale of books and broadside ballads. Everything emanating from the printing presses had to be licensed and recorded in the Company's registers and the appropriate fees paid. In 1588, the registration fee for a broadside ballad was fourpence.

The chapbooks and broadside ballads must surely have brightened up many lives, containing as they did not only many of the popular songs of the day but also the latest news, politics, love stories and murders. Pedlars would carry them in their packs, along with needles and pins and other necessities that countrywomen needed. The latest broadsides were pasted up in inn parlours and milkmaids pinned them on the dairy wall, where they then practised the popular songs while milking the cows. Sometimes the enterprising pedlar would offer to teach his customers the latest songs.

A medieval pedlar.

David Occomore, in his book *Curiosities of Essex*, writes:

> Elizabethan Essex did not escape the attention of ballad singers. Henry Chettle in his pamphlet Kind Hart's Dream of 1592, tells us of 'idle youths singing and selling ballads, in every corner of cities and market towns and especially at fairs and markets and such like public meetings.' Continuing: 'Now ballads are abusively chanted in every street and from London this evil has overspread Essex and the adjoining counties.
>
> Ballads, my masters, ballads. Will se ha' any ballads o' the newest and truest matter in all London. I have of them for all people and of all arguments, too. Here buy your story ballads, your nice maidens, your grave seniors and all sorts of men beside. Ballads! My master, rare ballads. Take a fine new ballad sir with a picture to 't.

Much of the content of the topical ballads was true for the most part, but often the facts were coloured by the ideas of the writer. And, of course, a good ballad seller could convince his public that anything in print was the truth.

The seventeenth century saw no improvement in the reputation of the ballad sellers and chapbook sellers. A number were found to be disreputable and in league with cutpurses who worked among the crowds that gathered around the seller in the streets and markets. In 1649, the magistrates were instructed to flog and imprison ballad sellers and confiscate their stock. These measures, along with religious and political unrest, led to a gradual decline and later partial collapse of the ballad trade.

Victorian England saw an upsurge in broadside ballad printing that was to overshadow earlier centuries. By the mid-1800s, the output of the printing presses was tremendous. Although London had the printing monopoly, there were several small family printing firms operating in Colchester and Rochford during Victorian times. Whenever a national event became news, the presses ran day and night to supply thousands of ballad sheets which were printed, packed and distributed to the pedlars who, being so close to London, were able to be on the Essex roads by dawn. They were eagerly bought by customers and pinned up in the inns and alehouses.

The most prolific output of material from local presses in Essex was at election times. A selection of these ballads has survived, if only to remind us that elections were at one time colourful affairs. 'New Song to an Old Tune' was issued by Mr J.B. Harvey of High Street, Colchester and refers to the 1847 election. This ballad mentions a number of prominent political figures of the day. Joseph A. Hardcastle (1815-1899), formerly of Writtle, was MP for Colchester from 1847 to 1852. Sir John T was Colonel John Tyssen Tyrell of Boreham House, who held one of the seats for the Conservatives in North Essex. Old Sir Henry refers to Sir George Henry Smyth of Berechurch Hall, who represented Colchester from 1826 to 1830. The line in the first verse. 'Have brought in a yellow and turned out a blue' alludes to the colours of the parties – yellow for the Whigs (Liberals) and blue for the Tories.

New Song to an Old Tune

Good news, said Jack Nokes to his neighbour Tom Stiles,
While quaffing their ale at a house in St Giles
For we Colchester Burgesses, trusty and true
Have brought in a Yellow, and turned out a Blue
Chorus: For the Rights of our Town
Our Country and Crown,
And the rights of our town.

What's in a Name?

Our county abounds with some interesting and curious names that appear on signposts and maps, fulfilling such an essential function in our everyday lives that we take them for granted. The 1½ million residents of Essex have almost 855,000 acres in their county and the name of every hamlet, village and town provides a folkloric clue, linking them to the heritage and history of our local landscape:

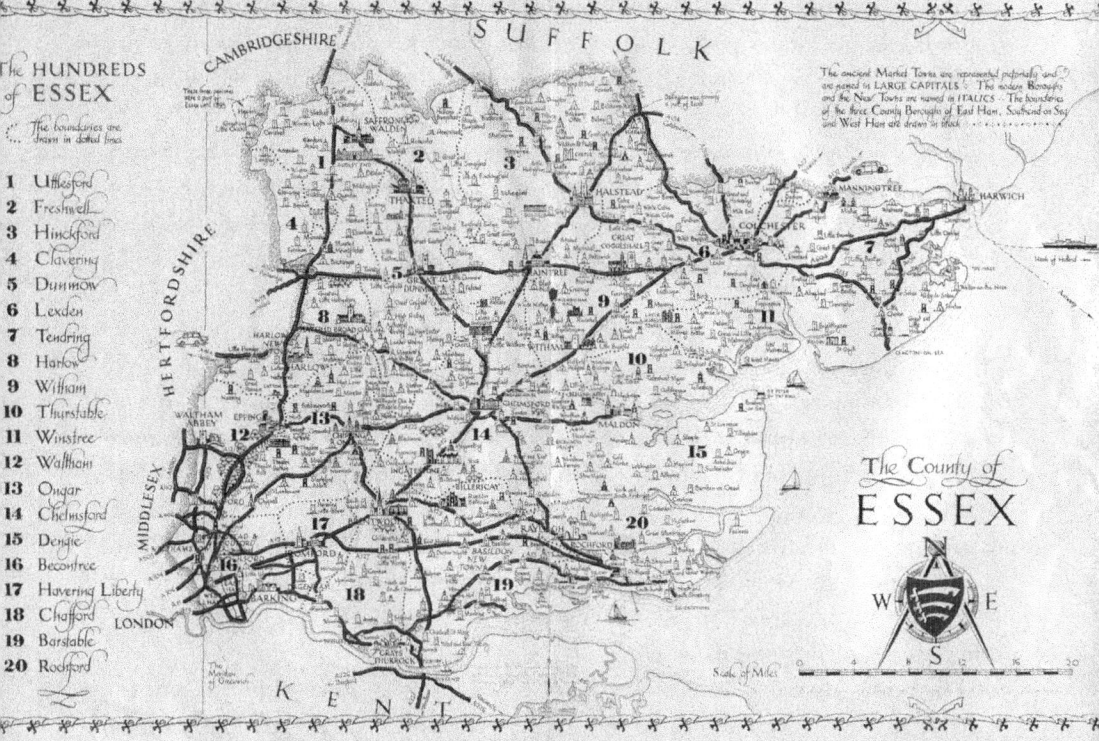

The famous Essex Hundreds map.

> Willingale Doe and Willingale Spain
> Bulphan and Bobbingworth, Colne-Engaine;
> Wenden Lofts, Beaumont-cum-Maze, Bung Row,
> Gestingthorpe, Ugley and Fingringhoe;
> Helions Bumpstead and Mountnessing,
> Bottle End, Tolleshunt D'Arcy, Messing
> Islands of Canvey, Foulness, Potton,
> Stondon Massey and Belchamp Otton;
> Ingrave and Inworth and Kedington,
> Shellow Bowels, Ulting and Kelvedon;
> Margaret Roothing and Manningtree –
> The bolder you sound 'em, the better they be.

These names, like the vast majority that appear in Reaney's *Book of Essex*, have original meanings that are not at all apparent from their modern forms. That is because most place names today are what could be termed 'linguistic fossils'. Although the names were used by our ancestors as descriptions of places, in terms of ownership, appearance, topography, use or other association, most have become mere labels, no longer possessing a clear linguistic meaning. This is perhaps not surprising when we consider that most place names are 1,000 years old or more.

A map printed in 1957 and specially drawn by Anthony New for *Essex Countryside* shows the ancient market towns with new towns and the twenty Hundreds of Essex, displaying a diversity of names emerging from British, Latin, Old English, Saxon, Norse and Norman French. Each of these languages has influenced the form of our existing place names and make a fascinating, but complicated, subject.

The Old English *ham*, in names such as Daecca's ham (Dagenham) generally means homestead, village, manor or estate and appears in more than thirty Essex place names; *ford*, meaning river crossing, appears in Romford; *ing* means a settlement of people, as in Barking (settlement of Berica's people); and *tun* or *ton*, as in Leyton, means farm or fenced enclosure, in this case by the river Lea. Epping was originally home to 'the people of the upland'. Ingatestone is one of a group of parishes south-west of Chelmsford which all take their name from a tribe called the Geringas. The use of this word implies an early Anglo-Saxon settlement in the area. The word *tye* (common) and *hatch* (gate) both crop up often, as does *ley* (wood or clearing).

The poet Edward Thomas loved the sounds of Essex places. He came to the county in 1915 when he joined the Artists' Rifles and was posted to Hare Hall Camp at Gidea Park. His family came also and they lived at nearby High Beech in Epping Forest. Off duty, Thomas explored the Essex countryside on his rusty old bike. Encouraged by his friend, the American poet Robert Frost, he began writing poetry, producing beautiful poems, many of which were published after his death in 1917 at the Battle of Arras in France. One trio of beautiful poems with Essex in mind begins:

> If I should ever by chance grow rich,
> I'll buy Codham, Cockridden and Childerditch,
> Roses, Pyrgo and Lapwater
> And let them all to my elder daughter,
> The rent I shall ask of her will be only
> Each year's first violets, white and lonely,
> The first primroses and orchises –
> She must find them before I do, that is.
> But if she finds a blossom on furze
> Without rent they shall all forever be hers,
> Whenever I am sufficiently rich:
> Codham, Cockridden and Childerditch
> Rose, Pyrgo and Lapwater
> I shall give them all to my elder daughter

Old Essex Sayings and Beliefs

Despite the sophistication of this modern world, Essex folk still seem to abide by an array of old sayings and superstitions to guide their lives. Some are connected to special times and events of the calendar, and no doubt many of them are confined to the older members of the county. Yet even younger people can usually reel off a repertoire of at least a few of the sayings they learned as children.

Here are just a few superstitions, known in other counties, but collected from Essex folk around the county:

Touch wood for good luck.
If you see a single magpie, hasten to spot another (one for sorrow, two for joy!).
It's bad luck to open an umbrella indoors.
Avoid passing a person on the stairs.
Bringing May blossom into the house brings bad luck.
Let someone else pick up your dropped glove.
Never put new shoes on a table.
Throw a pinch of salt over your left shoulder to counteract bad luck.
Avoid breaking a mirror – seven years of bad luck will follow.
If a purse is given as a gift, make sure to pop a silver coin within.
Never fail to pick up a pin – see a pin and pick it up and all day long you'll have good luck.
Do not kill a spider – if you wish to live and thrive, let the spider run alive.
Be mindful of giving scissors or knives as gifts – this could mean a friendship would be cut.
Friday the thirteenth is unlucky.
If the cat washes its face, rain is on the way.
Red sky at night, shepherds' delight, red sky at morning, shepherds' warning.
Whistling on board a boat could 'whistle up' a gale.
A black cat walking across your path is unlucky (conversely, lucky in some parts of Essex).
If bees stay close to their hives, rain is on the way.

For those who know weather lore, frost and snow in the winter months are not unwelcome at this time – farmers and gardeners need the cold weather to 'kill off the bugs and to break down the soil in readiness for spring harrowing'. Mild weather in any of the winter months – especially January – was once thought to be a very bad omen: 'Summer in winter, and a summer's flood, never boded England good' or 'A January spring is good for nothing!'

Ten

Music and Movement

Since singing is so good a thing, I wish all men would learn to sing.
William Byrd (1543-1623)

Folk Song

As the county dialect began to disappear, so too did the familiar songs and sayings of the region. Fortunately, at the beginning of the twentieth century, two special people came to the rescue. One was Dr Ralph Vaughan Williams (1872-1958), whose first visit to Essex was to influence his own compositions for the rest of his long life, and the other was Cecil Sharp (1859-1924). Both of them saved from extinction many of England's loveliest folk songs. The newly invented phonograph was available to record songs and music, some of which can be heard at the English Folk Dance and Song Society.

Vaughan Williams first came to Brentwood in 1903 at the invitation of Kate Bryan, the headmistress of the Montpelier School in Queens Road. She had organised a set of Oxford University-based lectures on folk song in which the thirty-one-year-old Vaughan Williams had recently become interested.

One of the students, forty-year-old Georgiana Heatley, known as Locksie, daughter of the rector of Ingrave, had also started collecting local songs from her father's parishioners. At the end of the fourth lecture given by Vaughan Williams in December 1903, she handed him a scrap of paper on which she had written a fragment of a song remembered from the time when she was a small child and it was sung to her by an old woman in Stambourne, deep in the Essex countryside.

Ralph Vaughan Williams as a young man, when he came to Ingrave.

The song was 'Cold Blow the Wind'. She invited the lecturer to a tea party for the old people of the village at her father's rectory at Ingrave, as she felt that some of them might be able to recall and sing songs of the past.

'This action started a "chain of destiny" for Vaughan Williams,' commented the late Frank Dineen, who wrote *The Ingrave Secret – Ralph's People* in 1998:

> Next day, the composer walked the three miles to Reverend Heatley's Rectory deep in the Brentwood countryside. There he was introduced to a 74-year-old shepherd, Charles Potiphar, whom Locksie and her sisters had heard sing lustily at previous Harvest Suppers. However, none of the old people, including Potiphar, could be persuaded to sing at this tea party.

This may have been because those present were mindful of the past tragedies that the eighty-three-year-old rector had suffered. The death of his wife Marian thirty-three years earlier, following the birth of their ninth child, and then the death of this baby and an older girl had far-reaching repercussions for him and his family. Parishioners believed that he had responded to these bereavements by making his children promise never to marry and they were all sensitive to the effects this sacrifice had on them. Potiphar was only too conscious that the best of the old songs he knew were about young love and sex, taboo subjects in the oppressive Victorian atmosphere of the rectory. Maybe seeing the disappointment on Vaughan Williams' face, Potiphar offered to sing to him next day at his home a quarter of a mile away in Rectory Lane.

Heatley's Rectory at Ingrave.

On Friday 4 December 1903, Vaughan Williams visited the old man's cottage in the alley that led south from Rectory Lane to St Nicholas's church, Ingrave. As he walked up the path, he found the old man, smiling and at ease in his smock, leaning against the timber doorframe of his cottage. Straight away, Potiphar launched into his favourite song, 'Bushes and Briars', a poignant country love song. 'The composer was entranced,' said Dineen:

> That single song had a tremendous impact on him. He was overwhelmed by the beauty of the words and melody and, as he wrote in his autobiography, this time at Ingrave influenced his subsequent style of composition. The thought that such songs could be lost forever turned him instantly into an enthusiastic collector.

Following that first meeting in Brentwood, Vaughan Williams returned again to Ingrave in January and February 1904. Over the next few months, he spent weeks cycling around Ingrave, Little Burstead, East Horndon and Billericay, and deeper into Essex, collecting songs. From the South East as a whole, he collected more than 800 songs and variations. In 1906, he revised the *English Hymnal* and used thirty-five to forty of the tunes he had found on his travels.

Throughout his long life, during which he composed much of our loveliest music for orchestra and film, Vaughan Williams often mentioned his fondness for Ingrave. In 1955, just a few years before his death, the great composer – now at the height of his fame – returned to Brentwood and recalled for his audience that first visit half a century earlier which had had such a profound influence on his life.

Essex Man

The centenary of the English Folk Dance and Song Society was celebrated at Cecil Sharp House in 1998. That year, Chingford's Tony Kendall was asked to publish his research in the book *Vaughan Williams: In Perspective*. Kendall, a prolific author, poet and composer, has written more than 1,000 songs, stories and poems with an Essex flavour and also plays fiddle for the Chingford Morris, as well as supporting the Good Easter Molly Gang.

During the 1970s, folklorists, scholars and county history enthusiasts realised that it was essential to make a determined effort to record the old Essex accents, telling the stories of long ago and singing the familiar songs before they and the older generation disappeared forever. So began the huge interest in preserving the remnants of our true Essex dialect by recording the voices of those Essex people. Although they are now just a memory, we can still hear them on tape and, in some rare cases, wax cylinder, at the Essex Record Office's Oral History Department in Chelmsford.

Let's Dance

Essex folk singers and dancers are grateful to Cecil Sharp, a contemporary of Vaughan Williams who was born in London in 1859. He was music master at Ludgrove School and his life's work of collecting folk material began in middle age. On Boxing Day 1899, Sharp saw the Headington Morris Dancers perform and noted down the tunes played on the concertina by William Kimber.

The centenary of Vaughan Williams' first visit to Essex. David Occomore, Tony Kendall and Sue Cubbin ERO.

At this time, Sharp did little more than arrange the tunes for piano. On a visit to Hambridge, Somerset in 1903, he overheard a gardener – John England – sing 'The Seeds of Love' and, like Vaughan Williams, became committed to a lifetime of collecting folk music.

At this time, at the beginning of the twentieth century, both men felt similarly that English music was being overshadowed by European styles. In 1908 Sharp wrote:

> In the village of today the polka, waltz and quadrille are steadily displacing the old-time country dances and jigs, just as the tawdry ballads and strident street-songs of the towns are no less surely exterminating the folk-songs.

In December 1911, Cecil Sharp founded the English Folk Dance Society at a public meeting. He continued collecting through the First World War, up until his death in 1924. The Society continued until 1932, when it amalgamated with the Folk Song Society (founded in 1898) to form the English Folk Dance and Song Society, whose headquarters are at Cecil Sharp House in London's Regent's Park Road.

On with the Dance

'On with the dance – let joy be unconfined' wrote Lord Byron, a regular visitor to South Weald in the early nineteenth century. Dancing in all its variations really does express joy and must always have had an uplifting effect on the spirit of Essex folk, from the simple jigs and step dancing practised by villagers to the more stately dances that were popular during the time of the Tudor court.

When entertaining Queen Elizabeth and her court during her frequent Progresses around Essex, her nobles were expected to provide music, masques and dancing. Woe betide the host if Elizabeth's favourite dances of the moment were not on the programme. Elizabeth is reported to have enjoyed the masques which were one of the earliest forms of theatre, developed from the ancient mumming and dance revels. These had been enjoyed by earlier monarchs and their court officials, who had extensive leisure time compared with the peasant classes that often worked themselves into early graves. The ancient masques grew in splendour during the early Stuart period, when nobles and rich commoners staged their own performances. The costumes, music and scenery became steadily more flamboyant over the years. Great merriment and excitement were created and the Wild Man, Neptune and other allegorical characters would give star performances.

A century later, Samuel Pepys, who was elected MP for Harwich in 1685, enjoyed the Essex countryside, but evidently not the dreadful state of the Essex Great Road. He often visited friends at Brentwood, Saffron Walden and, much

The beautiful Audley End.

further afield, Audley End. He seemed to enjoy his first visit to this beautiful house, which had been built in 1603, and upon arrival he recorded in his diary that 'this was exceedingly worth seeing' and that his host 'took us into the cellar, where we drank most admirable drink, a health to the king. Here I played on my flageolet, there being an excellent echo'.

A few years later, he recorded a ball in the presence of King Charles and Queen Catherine on 31 December 1662, mentioning a bransle and a courante, two fashionable dances of the day:

> very noble it was and a great pleasure to see the King leading the first which he called for: which was, says he, 'Cuckolds all a Row', the old dance of England.

Morris

The morris dance would have been familiar to Tudor monarchs, as it was the most widely-known ceremonial dance form in England. Its name is believed to derive from the Spanish *morisca* – a Moorish play or dance. Some historians believe it to derive from a much older ceremony. Common features were that the dancers were male, wore special costume and danced for display on special occasions.

The *Oxford Dictionary of English Folklore* suggests there are a brief number of references in fifteenth-century sources, the first known being in 1458. By 1494, at least, morris dancers were performing at the King's court:

> 2 January 1494: Privy purse expenses of Henry VII: For playing of the Mourice daunce £2 [and another on 4 February 1502].

In 1583, Philip Stubbes, that Puritan critic of 'Tudor fripperies', complained about the dancers 'bedecking themselves with scarfs, ribbons and laces, wearing bells on their legs, waving handkerchiefs over their heads and accompanied by hobby horses.'

By the end of the 1500s, morris dancing seems to have been popular entertainment and many writers of the time mentioned the dance. Shakespeare mentions a 'Whitsun morris-dance' in *Henry V* and Thomas Dekker created the play *The Shoemaker's Holiday*, in which the morris is performed by the shoemakers when entertaining the Lord Mayor.

In 1599, Will Kemp, a comedy actor and associate of William Shakespeare and 'a man of infinite jest', undertook to 'dance the Morrice' from London to Norwich – 127 miles away – where some of his family lived. He appears to have been a shrewd man and, with a period of unemployment looming (all theatres in London where closed by the Puritans for the Lenten forty days), he took up the wager to dance from London to Norwich.

This was a superb publicity stunt and an excellent way of earning money. At seven o'clock on Ash Wednesday, William Kemp set off from the Lord Mayor of London's house, accompanied by his friend Thomas Slye, a musician who played a pipe with one hand and beat a tabor (small drum) with the other. His servant, William Bee, and overseer, George Sprat, were also in the party. A huge crowd of people was there to see them off.

Kemp and a group of followers crossed over the old Bow Bridge into Essex and took their first rest. Luckily for historians, he kept a diary of his journey:

> Forward I went with my hey-de-gaies to Ilford where I again rested and was met by the people of the town and country thereabout very well welcomed, being offered carouses in the great spoon, one whole draught being able at that time to have drawn my little wit dry: but being afraid of the old proverb (he had need of a long spoon that eats with the devil), I soberly gave my boon companions the slip.

After dancing his way through Ilford, Kemp continued to Chadwell Heath, where, because it was getting dark, he ceased for that day. He was then given a lift on horseback into Romford, where he spent the night, probably at the Golden Lion, and rested the next day. Upon resuming, he was brought back to the spot in Chadwell Heath and made his way next to Brentwood, probably staying at the White Hart in the High Street. He arrived on market day at Brentwood on 14 February. Huge crowds had gathered at the marketplace in anticipation and, as Tom Slye played his pipe and tabor, Kemp danced for them all until he was exhausted. He then fought his way through the crowds to rest at the inn. Kemp wrote in his diary:

> In this town two cutpurses were taken, that with other two of their companions followed me from London as many better disposed people did. But these two dy-doppers gave out, when they were apprehended that they had laid wagers and betted

Will Kemp dancing his way from London to Norwich in 1600.

about my journey. Whereupon, the officers bringing them to my inn, I justly denied their acquaintance, saying that I remembered one of them to be a noted cutpurse, such a one as we tie to a post on our stage, for all people to wonder at when at a play, they are taking pilfering. This fellow and his half-brother being found with the deed, were sent to gaol; their two consorts had the charity of the town and after a dance at Trenchmore (a boisterous sort of dance to a lively tune in triple time) at the whipping cross, were sent back to London. Having rested well at Burnt Wood, the moon shining clearly and the weather being calm in the evening, I trippt it to Ingerstone.

When Kemp eventually reached Norwich – still dancing – a civic reception awaited him and he was presented with the sum of £5 and awarded an annual pension of 40s for life, a considerable sum at the time.

The following year, Kemp wrote a detailed account of his journey, which he described in his book *Nine Daies Wonder*. From the title, it has long been thought that the journey was accomplished in nine days but in fact it took twenty-seven because at various stages he took days off for resting – a total of eighteen in all. It was the actual dancing that took nine days. Nevertheless, it was a unique and remarkable performance.

To celebrate the 400th anniversary of Kemp's 'nine daies wonder', a re-enactment took place from 15-23 April 2000, involving many Essex morris sides and this challenging event was spectacularly successful.

Tony Motley as Will Kemp and Mike Oxenham as Thomas Slye, during the re-enactment of Kemp's 'nine daies wonder' in April 2000.

The Thaxted Morris Ring

The Thaxted Morris Men are Essex's oldest morris side, having been formed in 1911 by the wife of Thaxted's vicar, Conrad Noel. However, traditional morris dancing is thought to have been performed in the town in earlier years. On 2 June 1934, the famous Thaxted Morris Ring was founded. The Cambridge Morris Men invited five other sides, Letchworth, Thaxted, Oxford, East Surrey and Greensleeves, who met in Thaxted for the first Ring meeting. From that original group, there are now more than 250 sides throughout England, plus an Open Morris and Morris Federation, the latter two having women members.

The high point of the morris year is the annual gathering at Thaxted of morris men from all over England on the first weekend following the late May bank holiday. The ancient Abbots Bromley Horn Dance is performed late in the evening. This ancient hunting dance came to Thaxted many years ago. Some of the dancers carry horns. The simple tune, played by a lone fiddler, was collected in 1857 but the Abbots Bromley tradition could possibly date from the twelfth century. In 1960, Douglas Kennedy, the director of the English Folk Dance and Song Society, wrote in his book *England's Dances*:

> The Horn Dance ... casts its spell over the onlooker, not merely by the uncanny animal-like behaviour of the horn bearers. The slow jog-trot rhythm of the ten dancers, who wind in Indian file with measured and unhurried step, has its own hypnotic power. These animal-men trot in a manner that is dictated by the burden of the antlers pressing on their shoulders.

The Horn Dance at Thaxted, June 1960.

At the conclusion of their fascinating performance, the dancers in this picture (above) melted into single file and moved away in serpentine fashion and, shrouded in the outer darkness, slowly disappeared up Stony Lane while the haunting melody of the lovely old tune faded away with unearthly beauty on the night air.

Each morris side has its own distinctive style of dance and kit. Many Essex sides dance the Cotswold Morris, with its characteristic white handkerchiefs, sticks and bells. The Thaxted Morris Men wear red and white striped waistcoats, white trousers and decorated Panama hats. The Rumford Morris Men use the old spelling of Romford and its members have performed all over Essex since 1960. They dance mainly Cotswold Morris, with side members wearing blue and yellow baldricks with a bull's head logo and black breeches. Straw hats are worn and bell-pads are decorated with blue and yellow trim. They also perform Rapper Sword Dances from the north-east of England.

The Mayflower Morrismen of Billericay, formed in 1973, is the only side to wear black and white tabards, with the *Mayflower* ship on their back. Five of the Pilgrim Fathers, who sailed to America in 1620, came from Billericay, including the ship's governor. Contrasting with their sober kit, their hats are wonderfully decorated.

Mumming and Molly

Along with the morris, mummers' plays seem to have been popular from earliest records. They were performed in various places in the South East, such as Tendring, Pilgrims' Hatch and nearby South Weald, in 1903. In other parts of England, mummers were known as soulers and guisers. The Thameside Mummers have now collected thirty plays from all over the country and perform both locally and nationally.

Above: The Mayflower Morris men in their mumming play *St George and the Dragon*.

Left: A mumming play with the Bold Slasher and St George.

Traditionally, mummers had no need of props or scenery, as the idea was to move from one place to another over their planned route, performing just where they stood. Some mummers invariably wore jackets covered with long strips of coloured paper or material with their faces blackened. Disguise seemed to be more important than theatrical costume and many of the players blacked up with burnt cork. There were several themes around which the plays were enacted. The story of Robin Hood was often used as a theme for mummers' plays, but St George and the Dragon is probably the best known in Essex. It was performed at seasonal times such as Christmas and Boxing Day, as well as Plough Monday.

One of the reasons why mumming plays became less popular at the end of the nineteenth century was that they were purely an oral tradition. The themes were well known and the plays were acted out by local people and passed down the generations simply by learning the lines by heart, in the best tradition of folklore.

During the last decade, there has been a revival of the mumming play in Essex. In the town of Billericay, the Mayflower Morrismen performed their St George's Day mummers' play on 23 April, 2005 at several locations in the High Street. The script was a mixture of doggerel verse and prose and the subject was appropriately topical for that day, covering the combat between St George and the Turkish Knight. St George kills the knight, who is restored to life by the skills of a comic quack doctor. A feature of a number of mumming plays is the 'female' character, called Molly, Bessy or Mary. In this play, written by Julian Whybra, the female character was Sabra, the King of Egypt's daughter, played by Ross Holland. The accompanying music was played on the pipe and tabor by Mike Oxenham and on the accordion by Paddy Beadle.

Molly dancing, also performed by men, is the name by which morris was known in the east of England. It was known in East Anglia up until the Second World War. It appears that molly dancing, although similar, was not as complex as morris or sword dancing and has received much less attention. Molly dancers wore ordinary working clothes decorated with ribbons and rosettes and blackened their faces. The fullest reports of molly dancing come from the north-western parts at Great Chesterford and Helion Bumpstead.

The mollies danced vigorously in the village street, usually wearing their hobnailed working boots, and collected money from passers-by. Part of the custom was for the dancers to take a plough around the local village and if payment was not forthcoming they would cut a furrow across the householder's front lawn. There has been renewed interest in molly dancing over the last few years and the Good Easter Molly Gang are well known in Chelmsford and surrounding towns and villages.

Country Dance

In 1651, John Playford's *English Dancing Master* book, in which he collected and noted many of the early English folk dances, was published. It is not clear whether he made up the dances or simply published them from other sources. The book was published in eighteen further editions until 1728. More than most cultural forms, country dancing has moved up and down the social scale and has gone in and out of fashion, undergoing revivals at different times.

To combat the disappearing country dances from the village repertoire, the English Folk Dance and Song Society produced dedicated enthusiasts and dance teachers for whom country dancing at clubs, festivals and garden parties became normal hobby pursuits. It was Cecil Sharp who also succeeded in having country dance accepted on to the school curriculum and many schoolchildren who attended Essex schools in the years following the Second World War will today remember their weekly country dance lessons, in which the fascinating Sword Dance was performed to English country dance tunes.

Cecil Sharp began collecting English folk songs in 1903. Two years later, he had started composing an arrangement of folk dances when Mary Neal, a dance teacher, asked him if he knew of any she could teach to her students. His interest in folk dances led to the foundation of the Folk Dance Society in 1911. He interpreted the dances and helped English folk dance to become popular. Sharp's interest in folk songs took him to the Appalachian Mountains, where he studied American folk songs with English origins. Sharp was the foremost morris dance collector.

Throughout the 1930s and after the Second World War, many young people took up cycling and would meet at youth hostels around the county, where country dancing often became a highlight of the weekend's entertainment. Although country dance remained a favourite pastime of many enthusiasts, it had no appreciable effect on the mass popular culture, which took its various dance crazes from America. It was when Princess Margaret returned from a US trip in 1950 enthusiastically endorsing American square dance that the craze really took off in Essex. The dances were traditional, including squares, longways and circles, as were most of the tunes – jigs, reels, hornpipes and waltzes. These took place, with great enthusiasm, in the barns and village halls in just about every part of Essex.

Along with morris, molly and sword dancing, numerous other kinds of dancing clubs sprang up in Essex, including Scottish and Irish ceilidhs, Appalachian, ladies' clog dancing, jive and, of course, the current line dancing, borrowed from America a decade ago.

The ceilidh, originally a Gaelic social gathering including song, music, storytelling and dance, both social and display, is popular throughout Essex, with the Grand Ceilidh Club holding their weekly meeting in Southend.

There was once a lack of dance material but Essex can feel particularly proud of its connection with many distinguished song and dance collectors, musicians and composers who lived and worked in the county during past centuries.

Music Makers

From way back in the sixteenth century, Essex has played a significant part in the musical heritage of Britain. At the time of the Dissolution of the monasteries in 1540, the composer and organist Thomas Tallis was organist at Waltham Abbey and had the honour of being appointed one of the Gentlemen of the Chapel Royal. Known as the Father of English church music, some of his hymn tunes, including 'Glory to Thee, my God', are still in general use today.

For thirty years, Stondon Massey was the home of William Byrd (1543-1623), the remarkable composer often referred to as Stondon's Master of Music. Byrd's compositions covered the whole range of contemporary music – madrigals, solo songs, canons, rounds, instrumental music for virginals and strings, and, above all, church music. His association and affection for Tallis, with whom he shared duties as organist at the Chapel Royal, was shown in his comment that he had been 'bred up to music under Thomas Tallis'.

Thaxted was the village chosen by Gustav Theodore Holst (1874-1934) when he came to live in Essex in 1917. He resided at Monk Street, Town Street and in 1925 moved to a large Elizabethan house at Brook End. Holst studied composition under Stanford at the Royal College of Music. At first, he was influenced by the music of Grieg, then by Bach and Wagner, and in later life by English folk song and Tudor composers. In 1903, he gave up his career as a trombone player to write music and became director of music at St Paul's School, which for some years remained a welcome refuge for a diffident man who shunned fame and popularity. It was while living at Monk Street, Thaxted that he wrote that most evocative of twentieth-century classics, *The Planets*, a suite for orchestra. Holst's daughter Imogen, who inherited much of her father's musical talent, was a great companion to her father during the last years of his life.

One-time resident and rector of the East Mersea parish for ten years was the prolific composer, hymn writer and author the Revd Sabine Baring-Gould (1834-1924), who famously composed 'Onward Christian Soldiers' in 1864. In collaboration with Cecil Sharp, Baring-Gould published *English Folk Songs for Schools* in 1906 and contributed greatly to the world of folk-song and music.

Number 1 High Street, Harlow was the birthplace of Sarah Fuller in 1805. She wrote the hymn 'Nearer My God to Thee' and 'Darkness Shrouded Calvary'. Her sister, who was two years older, set the words to music.

Jane Taylor of Chipping Ongar (1783-1824) came from an extraordinarily gifted family, who produced artists, engravers, inventors and authors. Jane was a precocious child, writing from the age of eight, alone or with her sister Ann. Together with their father, they produced the very popular *Original Poems for Infant Minds* in 1805, which includes 'My Mother' by Ann, who later wrote 'Meddlesome Matty'. More poems followed, notably 'Twinkle, Twinkle Little Star' by Jane. Her verse was admired by Scott, her prose by Browning.

John Ireland (1879-1962), one of England's greatest twentieth-century composers, stayed at Little Sampford in 1941 and occupied a wing of the rectory until 1945.

Arthur Henry Brown (1830-1926) was one of England's most accomplished composers of hymns and church music. Born in Crown Street, Brentwood, he showed incredible musical ability by being appointed organist at St Thomas' church at the age of ten. During his long life, he composed more than 1,000 hymn tunes, many of which gained worldwide popularity, including 'Saffron Walden', the tune he wrote for 'Just As I Am'. The famous 'O Love Divine' was written one Sunday morning in fifteen minutes, just before the service. His main compositions are to be found in most of the principal hymnals of today.

Eleven

Legendary Folk

Perhaps, of all the counties of England, the one which is least known by English people generally is the county of Essex.

Frances C. Burmester, *John Lott's Alice*, 1902

Much regional folklore is clustered around real people and the historical events in which those people were involved during their lifetimes. Fact and fable are entwined in the stories of some of our celebrated – and notorious – Essex characters.

Roman Generals

During the late Iron Age, the people of southern Britain were divided into separate tribes or kingdoms. Each kingdom had its own ruler and in the area which was to become Essex, the Trinovantes tribe was established in what we now know as modern Colchester. The area then covered was about 12 square miles (32 square kilometres).

In 55 BC, Julius Caesar, having conquered most of Gaul (France), turned his attention to Britain and invaded with five legions and cavalry in a fleet of more than 800 vessels. He stayed but a short time, returning the following year after penetrating through Essex and onward into the area now known as Hertfordshire.

Cunobelin was the ruler of both the Trinovantes and the neighbouring Catuvellauni and reigned from around 5 BC to AD 40, the year of his death. The Roman historian Suetonius observed that Cunobelin was held in high regard by the Romans, not as a simple tribal leader but as *Rex Britannorum*, King of the Britons, the inspiration for many folk stories. The extent of his power spread even further, as is seen through his gold coins which have been found all over south-east Britain. Shakespeare was inspired to use this character in his great play *Cymbeline*.

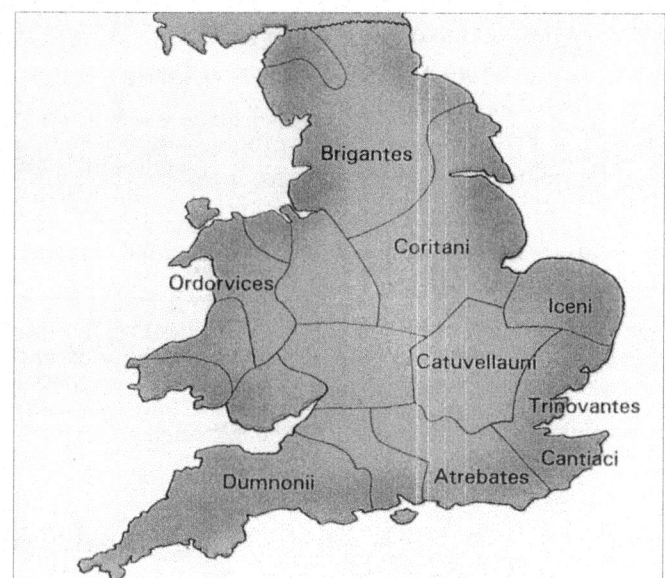

A map showing the pre-Roman tribes.

A Roman soldier on duty at the Colchester Castle Museum, 2004.

By AD 41, Claudius had become Emperor of Rome and within two years had sent an army to Britain, led by General Aulus Plautius. The 50,000-strong army landed in Kent; their objective was the capture of Colchester (known as *Camulodunum*). During their march northwards, they fought many Britons, including Cunobelin's two sons, Caratacus and Togodumnus; the latter was killed in battle.

Before the coming of the Romans, when a large part of the country was dense forest, there were no roads in Britain in the accepted sense, nor were there towns. Along the route from London to Colchester, Roman stations were established. One, named *Durolitum*, was between Romford and Brentwood, possibly at Gidea Park; another, *Caesaromagus*, was at Chelmsford and a third, named *Canonium*, is believed to have been at either Kelvedon or Rivenhall. As the Roman army approached Colchester, Claudius arrived from Italy to take charge of the attack on this important British stronghold. They captured the Iron Age capital accompanied by elephants – which the Britons would not have seen before. That invasion began a 400-year occupation of Britain and is a significant part of our history.

Boudica

We can thank the Roman historian Tacitus for his chronicles, which include an account of the relatively short time that Queen Boudica and her husband King Prasutagus ruled their tribe of native Britons, the Iceni, in the area of modern Norfolk and north Suffolk. King Prasutagus had been a willing link with the Romans but on his death in AD 60, the land belonging to the Iceni was violently annexed by the Roman leaders. Despite promises that had been made to Prasutagus, Boudica was assaulted and her two daughters violated.

Boudica statue at Westminster Bridge.

So great was her anger that in AD 61 she raised the whole of south-east England in revolt and before the main Roman armies could return from campaigning in Wales, she burned *Londinium* (London), *Verulamium* (St Albans) and *Camulodunm* (Colchester). The present Colchester Castle is built on the site of the Temple of Claudius, where there are still charred remains left as a reminder. In all, about 70,000 people were killed before the Roman governor Suetonius Paulinus was able to defeat the Britons and crush the rising.

The Iceni were virtually annihilated and Boudica met her end. Exactly how this happened, we will probably never know. Some historians have theorised that she poisoned herself and her daughters shortly before the glowing embers of Colchester had died down. However, there are also claims that she died elsewhere in Essex.

King Coel

Geoffrey of Monmouth, writing in the twelfth century, tells us about King Coel (of nursery rhyme fame), who lived and ruled over Colchester, England's oldest recorded town. Supposedly, his daughter Helena was the mother of the Roman emperor Constantine (AD 306-337). It is said that Colchester Castle was built upon King Coel's palace, the site of the Temple of Claudius which had been destroyed by Boudica centuries earlier. According to legend, King Coel led a revolt against the Romans and made himself ruler of Essex. Constantius was sent to suppress the rising but while laying siege to Colchester he met Helena and was so affected by her beauty that he made peace with Coel, her father, in order to marry her.

Helena was said to have adopted Christianity when Constantine Augustus made it the official religion of the Roman Empire by the Edict of Milan. She went on a pilgrimage to Jerusalem, where, according to the legend, she discovered the cross of Christ. This is commemorated in the arms of Colchester, and the earliest seal of the bailiffs bears her image. Although without foundation, Helena is regarded as the patron saint of Colchester.

Holy Folk

For all the early efforts of the Romans, Britain was still chiefly a land of thick forest, marsh and fen, and by AD 410 the Roman Eagle, which had arrived so proudly to Essex's shores and which had stood firmly as a symbol of authority, was gone. For over 100 years, Britain was prey to invasions from many different foreign tribes, but by AD 527 the pagan Saxons were well established and the land of the East Saxons – which gave the county its name – has endured for nearly

1,500 years. Around twenty-six kings reigned in Essex between AD 580 and AD 840. Exact dates are hard to establish but by the time Essex emerged as a kingdom, both London and Colchester had been resettled and both lay within its borders.

In AD 596, Pope Gregory sent monks to Britain to convert the people to Christianity. Within a year, Augustine – who later became a saint – had converted the pagan king of Kent, Ethelbert, to Christianity and valuable land at Canterbury was granted to Augustine. Canterbury was to play a vital part in the life of Essex pilgrims in following centuries and many miracles were believed to be attributable to these early monks.

In around AD 600, England was divided into a septarchy – seven kingdoms. The names and descent of the East Saxon kings are known but very little else. In AD 666, the monk Erkenwald built an abbey at Barking at the request of his sister Ethelburga, who became its first abbess. Barking Abbey was probably the first nunnery established in England for women and was to become one of the richest and most important. Erkenwald was the grandson of the King of the East Angles and was the first bishop to preach in St Paul's, London.

St Cedd, a monk of Lindisfarne in Northumbria, came as missionary bishop to Essex. He founded a monastery at Tilbury but lived at Bradwell-juxta-Mare, where he built the church of St Peter-on-the-Wall, on the inner wall of the ruined fortress of Othona. The Jarrow monk Bede, the first notable English historian, described how Cedd's missionary work spread and gathered 'much Church, great Church, to the Lord'. St Peter-on-the-Wall was the first of many churches to be built in Saxon Essex.

St Peter-on-the-Wall at Bradwell.

St Osyth

Osyth was a Saxon saint whose name is perpetuated in this lovely village by the sea. The legend tells us that she was the daughter of Redwald, the first Christian King of the East Angles, and his wife, Wilburga. Many tales of Osyth's goodness are recorded. One tells of the time she fell into a river and was drowned, but was restored to life by the prayers of St Modwen, her tutor.

After being reunited with her parents, she married Sighere, King of the East Saxons. But before the marriage was consummated, she took the veil. Sighere, accepting her vocation, gave her his village of Chich and founded an abbey there with Osyth as abbess. In AD 653, Danish pirates landed near Chich and, after burning the surrounding countryside, attacked Osyth's abbey, forcing the nuns to accept their pagan gods. When Osyth refused, she was beheaded but, according to the writer Thomas Fuller, so sainted and pure was she that: 'Yet this head after it was cut off, was carried by St Osyth (Oh, wonder! Oh, lie!) three furlongs and then she fell down and died.' In Nun's Wood, near the priory, the ghostly figure of poor decapitated St Osyth is supposed to walk, holding her head in one hand.

Byrhtnoth

Maldon is first mentioned in AD 912 in the *Anglo-Saxon Chronicle*. Maldon was a borough by the time of the Domesday Book in 1086. Danish and Norse raiders would regularly descend on the Essex coast. The Earl (ealdorman) of Essex, Byrhtnoth, led more than 1,000 men out to defend Maldon against a huge Viking army camped on Northey Island. Having allowed the Vikings to cross to the mainland before giving battle, the Saxons were overwhelmed and Byrhtnoth was killed. The Vikings took away his head. One of the earliest surviving English epic poems included in the *Anglo-Saxon Chronicle* records the disaster. A statue of Byrhtnoth was erected on All Saints church in Maldon in 1907.

King Harold

The Bayeux Tapestry gives us a fascinating glimpse of the life and death of that last brave Saxon monarch, King Harold II, who died on the battlefield at Hastings on 14 October 1066. Many towns have laid claim to being the last resting-place of King Harold, but according to William Andrews, in his book *Bygone Essex* (1892):

> The place of interment of the last of the Saxon monarchs is a subject much controverted in the present day. Many historians appear to be entirely opposed to the most authentic versions of the story; that Harold was buried at Waltham Holy Cross.

Byrhtnoth, the Saxon Ealdorman of Essex, who fought at the Battle of Maldon in AD 991.

Peasants' Revolt

The court rolls of Great Canfield, Blackmore and Birdbrook all refer to the Black Death of 1349, which carried away one-third of the county's population. No longer were there enough labourers in Essex to carry on farming and the peasants, still bound to their lords, resented the crippling poll taxes imposed to raise money for the war against France.

On 30 May 1381, the peasants of Essex attacked the King's commissioner, who came to Brentwood to investigate the tax returns. The uprising spread rapidly and the peasants began burning the evidence of their villeinage. At Coggeshall, they plundered the manor house and at Cressing Temple they burned Sir Robert Hales' home. Uniting with commoners from Kent, the rebels marched to London, by which time they numbered 100,000. Jack Straw, Wat Tyler and John Ball influenced the rebels and all were betrayed by the young Richard II, who when meeting with them at Mile End on 14 June agreed to their demands. They asked for an end to serfdom, the fixing of low rents and an unconditional pardon. Once the threat posed by the revolt had been lifted, Richard withdrew his promise. Five hundred peasants fled to Billericay, where they were savagely killed by soldiers in Norsey Wood. Jack Straw and Wat Tyler were executed and their heads placed on poles on London Bridge.

Lady Jane Grey

In the sixteenth century, the Manor of Woodham Ferrers belonged to the parents of Lady Jane Grey, born in 1537. Jane's father was Henry Grey, the Marquis of Dorset and Duke of Suffolk. Jane and her two sisters, Catherine and Mary, were great-granddaughters of Henry VII.

In 1553, the Duke of Northumberland, foreseeing the early death of Edward VI, aimed to secure the succession of the English throne by arranging for the marriage of Jane to his fourth son, Lord Guildford Dudley on 21 May, 1553. Following Edward's death on 9 July, 1553, Jane was named as his successor. But after just nine days as Queen of England, she was forced to abdicate in favour of Princess Mary, daughter of Henry VIII, who had popular support. Jane was imprisoned in the Tower of London and beheaded on Tower Green.

The historian, Thomas Fuller, in his Book of Worthies, described Lady Jane Grey: 'She had the birth of a princess, the learning of a divine, the life of a saint, yet died the death of a malefactor for the offences of her parents.'

Queen Elizabeth I

Most people in Elizabethan Essex must have seen their Queen at some time, as she seemed to have enjoyed travelling on Progresses around Essex, where she passed through small villages. The Essex Great Road would have been familiar to her. She is recorded as having slept in at least 240 different places during her forty-four-year reign, many in Essex

She often visited the ancient boroughs of Colchester, Maldon, Harwich and Saffron Walden. New Hall, Boreham, was a favourite, as this lovely manor house was built by her father, King Henry VIII, in 1517, and she also visited the Altham family at Mark Hall, Latton, several times.

The Earl of Leicester entertained the Queen at Wanstead House and Sir William Petre at Ingatestone Hall was a favourite host, as was Sir Thomas Mildmay at Moulsham. She visited the great houses at Loughton, Epping, Great Hallingbury, Gosfield, Ongar and Kelvedon. At Horham Hall, Thaxted, she stayed for as long as nine days in 1571.

Elizabeth's most famous visit to Essex did not form part of a regular Progress. In 1588, when her sailors were fighting the Spanish Armada, she went by water to Tilbury, reviewed her troops and delivered her noblest speech:

> Let tyrants fear: I have always so behaved myself that under God, I have pleased my chiefest strength and safeguard in the loyal hearts and goodwill of my subjects; and therefore I am come amongst you, as you see, at this time, not for my recreation and disport, but being resolved, in the midst and heat of the battle, to live or die amongst

you all, to lay down for my God, and for my kingdoms and for my people, my honour and my blood, even in the dust.

Dick Turpin

Hempstead was the place of birth in 1705 of Richard Turpin. He was apprenticed to a butcher in London's Whitechapel and later owned a butcher shop. Then he began stealing cattle, followed by a spell of smuggling. Soon he was a member of the dreaded criminal Gregory Gang. Around 1735, they were robbing remote farmhouses. The *London Gazette* reported on 7 June 1737 that Turpin was 'the famous highwayman' who 'used the passengers with a great deal of civility'. However, reports of his cruelty and torture of old people who could not defend themselves compelled George II to offer a £50 reward for his capture.

When local constables captured two of the gang, Turpin headed to Epping Forest, where he lived in a cave and began working with Tom King, a well-known highwayman. So notorious was Turpin that another bounty of £100 was placed on his head – a reward that unwittingly transformed him from common footpad into a murderer. On 4 May 1737, a gamekeeper named Morris tracked Turpin to Epping Forest. When challenged at gunpoint, Turpin drew his own gun and shot Morris dead.

Turpin then lived rough in Epping Forest. Realising that if he remained in Essex he could not escape capture, he set off to live in Yorkshire under the name of John Palmer, financing his lifestyle with excursions into Lincolnshire for occasional highway robbery. One day, returning from an unsuccessful hunt, he shot his landlord's rooster. When the landlord complained, he threatened to kill the landlord too. He was taken into custody while local authorities made enquiries as to how exactly 'Mr Palmer' made his money. Imprisoned in York Castle dungeons, while charges were investigated, he stupidly wrote to his brother, requesting him to 'procure an evidence from London that could give me a character that would go a great way towards my being acquitted'.

Unfortunately for Turpin, his brother was too mean to pay the sixpence postage due and so returned the letter to the post office. By coincidence, Turpin's former schoolmaster recognised the handwriting. Showing the letter to the local magistrate, they opened it and despite the fact that it was signed John Palmer, the writer was identified as Turpin.

Turpin was sentenced to death. Pleas from his father to have the sentence commuted to transportation fell on deaf ears. Between his sentence and execution, visitors frequented Turpin's cell. He bought new clothes and hired five mourners for 10s each. On 19th April 1739, Dick Turpin rode through the streets of York in an open cart, bowing to the crowds. At York racecourse, he climbed the ladder to the gibbet and then sat for half an hour chatting to the guards and the executioner.

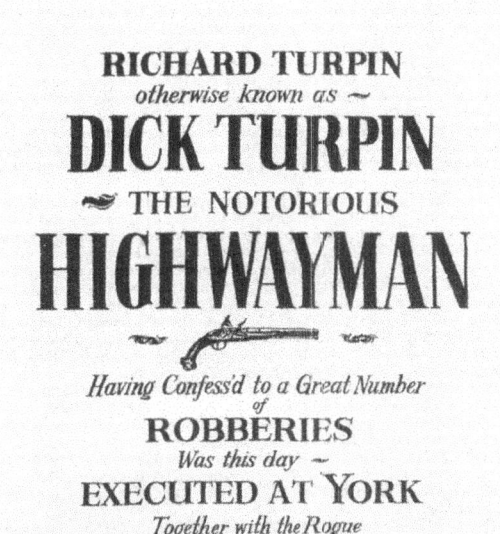

A poster depicting Dick Turpin's deeds.

An account of Turpin's execution in the *York Courant* on 19 April 1739 notes his brashness even at the end: 'with undaunted courage looked about him, and after speaking a few words to the topsman, he threw himself off the ladder and expired in about five minutes.' Thus, in death at least, Turpin attained some of the gallantry that had eluded him in life.

Lionel Lukin

Great Dunmow was the birthplace of Lionel Lukin, born in 1742. Here, in 1785, Lukin developed and tested the first 'unimmergible boat' on the local pond, lodging his patent for an 'improved method of construction of boats ... for either sailing or rowing, which will neither overset in violent gales ... nor sink by any accident when filled with water'. A month later, the patent was granted to Lukin, who rightly claimed the credit for the invention of the lifeboat which ever since has saved so many people's lives. He was a personal friend of the Prince Regent, later George IV, who encouraged the inventor to develop his ideas. He retired in 1824, a significant year that saw the founding of the National Institute for the Preservation of Life from Shipwreck, later to become the familiar Royal National Lifeboat Institution.

King George III

Brentwood was a place of excitement on 19 October 1778. That day King George III, the staunchest of Protestant kings, and Queen Charlotte passed through the town on a visit to Lord Petre, one of the most eminent of Roman Catholic peers. The townspeople gave their monarchs a tumultuous welcome and the road from the town to Thorndon Hall, Lord Petre's new mansion, was lined with soldiers. Later, there was a wonderful party with fireworks and a concert. Next day, the King rode over to Warley, reviewed his troops and witnessed a mock battle. When he departed, he handed Lord Petre 100 guineas for the Thorndon servants and left money for the poor of Brentwood.

Elizabeth Fry

Plashet at East Ham was the Essex village that was home for a while to Elizabeth Fry (1780-1845). At a time when it was unthinkable for a women to be anything but a subservient wife and mother, Elizabeth Fry (*née* Gurney) entered the male preserve of public life.

Elizabeth is best known for her prison reforms, although she also campaigned for improved conditions in asylums and hospitals. She was also involved in the promotion of training of nurses and organised shelter for London's homeless. Elizabeth experienced a religious conversion after hearing a sermon by the American Quaker William Savery in 1798 and devoted her life to preaching and ministering to the poor. She married a fellow Quaker, Joseph Fry, and they produced eleven children. Her great friend, Elizabeth Hanbury, born in Essex in 1793, lived in three centuries, dying in 1901.

James Banyard

James Banyard's name is still well known in Tillingham where, in 1838, the Rochford-born shoemaker founded the religious sect that became the Chapel of the Peculiar People. By 1900, Essex had more than forty such places of worship. The word 'peculiar' originally meant 'special' in the biblical sense and there are several references in the Old Testament.

Preaching his own brand of elemental Methodism in his cramped cottage or in the open air in the Rochford market square, Banyard's followers gradually increased. At first his fiery evangelistic message was met with derision. However, within a few years, other chapels were opened throughout Essex, including Herongate, Fobbing, Great Wakering, South Green and, of course, Tillingham. This is the only Peculiar Chapel still following the old service in the Essex countryside. In 1956, the Peculiar People's church was absorbed into the Union of Evangelical Churches.

The Peculiar People enjoying a celebration tea at Chelmsford.

John Constable

East Bergholt, Suffolk was the place of birth of John Constable on 11 June, 1776. He was educated at Dedham Grammar School, Essex and here was encouraged by Sir George Beaumont, the Essex patron of artists. He loved Dedham Vale, which was the scene of so many of his lovely paintings. In 1821, he wrote: 'I associate my careless boyhood with all that lies on the banks of the Stour. Those scenes made me a painter, and I am grateful – that is, I had often thought of pictures before I ever touched a pencil.'

Guglielmo Marchese Marconi

When thinking of Chelmsford, the first name that comes to mind is Marconi. In 1896, the twenty-two-year-old scientist took out his first patent for 'transmitting electrical impulses and signals'. In the following year, at Chelmsford, he founded his Wireless Telegraph Co. and built his first factory. Here, associates carried out most of the early research which enabled him, in 1901, to hear in Newfoundland the first Morse messages sent across the Atlantic from his transmitting station in Cornwall. Wireless equipment made at the Chelmsford works and constantly improved by the Marconi scientists was fitted first to ships and then to aircraft. After the First World War, the Marconi company, using the short-wave beam system, established a worldwide Imperial telegraph service. At Chelmsford, the first sound broadcast took place on 15 June, 1920 and listeners heard the voice of the famous singer, Dame Nellie Melba.

Lord Byron often stayed at Gilstead Hall in South Weald.

Lord Byron

The weekend visits of Lord Byron to South Weald's elegant Wealdside, (later Gilstead Hall) during the early eighteenth century caused much excitement to the household of Mr James Hanson, Byron's solicitor and great friend from the time Byron succeeded to the barony as a ten-year-old.

Hanson had bought Wealdside in 1813. Byron, who by then was a successful poet, was leading a colourful life in London society. Lady Carolyn Lamb had described him as 'mad, bad and dangerous to know'. Following publication of his epic poem, *Childe Harold's Pilgrimage,* his verses were seized on as fast as they were published. Byron's fondness for the Hanson family was evident when, on 7 March 1814, he gave Mary Ann Hanson away at her wedding to Lord Portsmouth. Byron also made the solicitor one of his executors and in his last will left him the sum of £1,000. Wealdside has had many owners over the years and several sightings of Lord Byron's ghost have been reported in the grounds.

Edwin Dunning

The church of Bradfield overlooks the estuary of the river Stour and, like older Essex churches, is steeped in history. However, inside it contains a dedication to a man of the village. He was Squadron Commander Sir Edwin Harris Dunning DSC RN. On 2 August 1917, at the height of the First World War, he landed an aircraft on a vessel underway, the first person to do so. This legendary feat changed the way that air power could be delivered by sea to all parts of the world. In St Lawrence's church is a plaque and a stained-glass window in his honour and also dedicated to the Royal Flying Corps and to his ship, HMS *Furious*. Edwin Dunning was killed five days later.

BIBLIOGRAPHY

Addison, Sir William, *Essex Worthies*, Phillimore, 1973
Allingham, Marjorie, *The Oaken Heart*, Isis, 1999
Andrews, William, *Bygone Essex*, SR Publications, 1969
Astbury, A.K., *Estuary*, Carnforth Press, 1980
Austin, Geoff, *Another Miller's Tale*, Mountnessing Parish Council, 1994
Baker, Margaret, *Folklore & Customs of Rural England*, David & Charles, 1974
Barnes, Alison, *Folklore Medicine*, Essex Countryside, 1992
Beckett, R.A., *Romantic Essex 1901*, PBK Publishing, 2001
Bensusan, S.L., *Back of Beyond*, Blandford Press, 1988
Brand, John, *Popular Antiquities & Great Britain*, John Russell Smith, 1870
Bridges, Zoe, *Barefoot & Buttonhooks*, self-published, 1992
Christy, Miller, *The Mineral Waters & Medicinal Springs of Essex*, Essex Field Club, 1910
Clamp, Frances, *Essex Living Memories*, Frith, 2002
Cooper, Ashley, *Heart of our History*, Bulmer Historical Society, 1994
Crancher, Steve, *Dijja Wanna Say Sumfing?*, Ian Henry Publications, 2002
Deacon, Richard, *Matthews Hopkins: Witch finder General*, Frederick Muller Ltd, 1976
Duff, Gail, *The Wheel of the Wiccan Year*, Rider & Co., 2002
Evans, Brian, *Romford, Collier Row and Gidea Park*, Phillimore, 1994
Gardiner, Tom, *Broomsticks over Essex*, Ian Henry Publications, 1981
Gascoigne, Margaret, *English Customs and Traditions*, Shire Publications, 1998
Gepp, Edward, *Essex Dialect*, SR Publishing, Yorkshire, 1920
Gunby, Norman, *A Potted History of Ilford*, self-published, 1997
Hole, Christina, *English Traditional Customs*, B.T. Batsford, 1975
Johnstone, Michael, *Anniversary Celebrations*, Ward Lock, 1988
Jones, Alison, *The Wordsworth Dictionary of Saints*, Chambers, 1992
Kent, Sylvia, *Brentwood – A Photographic History*, Black Horse Books, 2002
Laurie, Peter, *The Tyrrells of Heron*, Wilson & Whitworth, 1900
Le Vay, Benedict, *Eccentric Britain*, Bradt Publications, 2000
Loftus E. and H. Chettle, *A History of Barking Abbey*, Wilson & Whitworth, 1900
Lovell, Keith, *History Though Essex*, Vol. 1, Keith Lovell Publications, 1997
Manser, Martin, *Dictionary of Word & Phrase Origins*, Sphere Books Ltd, 1990
McIntyre, Anne, *Folk Remedies for Common Ailments*, Gaia Books, 1994
Mee, Arthur, *The King's England – Essex*, King's England Press, 1991

Mills West, H., *East Anglia: Tales of Mystery & Murder*, Countryside Books, 2000
Mills, A.D., *English Place-Names*, Oxford University Press, 1991
Morant, Philip, *The History and Antiquities of the County of Essex*, 1768
Occomore, David M., *Curiosities of Essex*, Ian Henry Publications, 1984
Payne, Jessie K., *A Ghosthunter's Guide to Essex*, Ian Henry Publications, 1987
Pegg, Bob, *Rites and Riots*, Blandford Press, 1981
Pennick, Nigel, *The Subterranean Kingdom*, Capall Bann Publishing, 2001
Pewsey, Lynn, *A Taste of Essex*, Ian Henry Publications, 1994
Phillips, Roger, *Wild Food*, Pan Books Ltd, 1983
Phelps, Humphrey, *An Essex Christmas*, Alan Sutton, 1993
Pickering, David, *Dictionary of Superstitions*, Cassells Publishing, 1996
Porter, Enid, *Folklore of East Anglia*, B.T. Batsford, 1974
Potter, Carol, *Touchwood*, Guild Publishing, 1990
Pusey, Richard, *Essex: Rich and Strange*, Hale Publishing, 1987
Puttick, Betty, *Ghosts of Essex*, Countryside Books, 1997
Richman, Harry, *Billericay and its High Street*, CPRE, 1953 and 1963
Roe, Fred, *Essex Survival*, Methuen, 1929
Saltmarsh, C. and N. Jennings, *Havering Village to Harold Wood*, Phillimore, 1995
Seymour, John, *Forgotten Household Crafts*, Dorling Kindersley, 1987
Simpson, Jacqueline and Steve Roud, *A Dictionary of English Folklore*, Oxford University Press, 2003
Sipple, Mavis, *Extraordinary Essex*, Brent Publications, 2000
Steer, Francis W., *The History of the Dunmow Flitch Ceremony*, Essex Record Office, 1951
Streeter, D. and R. Richardson, *Discovering Hedgerows*, BBC Publications, 1982
Sykes, Homer, *Mysterious Britain*, Orion, 1993
Thomas, Richard, *Larn Yoursel Essex Dialect*, Nostalgia Publications, 1999
Wallace, Elizabeth, *Extraordinary Places – Close to London*, Hastings House, 2004
Weightman, Gavin, *The Seaside*, Spire Books, 1991
Wentworth Day, James, *Book of Essex*, Egon Publishing, 1979
West, H. Mills, *East Anglia: Tales of Mystery & Murder*, Countryside Books, 2000

INDEX

Adam, Brother 79, 81
Addison, Sir William 113
Advent 69
Ainge, Revd Canon David 13
Ainsworth, William Harrison 12
Ale-conner 102
Allen, Benjamin 80
Anne, Queen 14, 19, 93
Armistice 68
Ash Wednesday 52, 166
Ashingdon 129
Audley End 165
Bailey, Sheila 52, 55
Banyard, James 184
Bard, Mary 13
Baring-Gould, Revd Sabine 173
Barking 19, 36, 53, 66, 89, 90, 99, 120, 142, 152, 158, 178
Barking Abbey 36, 178, 138
Barnes, Alison 74, 138
Barnum, Phineas Taylor 116
Bartlett, Jack 67
Basildon 57, 113, 128, 129, 152
Baxter, Eva 52, 69, 83
Bayeux Tapestry 179
Beating the bounds 58
Beadle, Paddy 171
Bedloe, Thomas 74
Beer-making 102, 103, 104
Bell, The (Horndon-on-the-Hill) 54
Beltane 56, 66
Berden 25, 99

Betjeman, Sir John 11
Billericay 48, 54, 55, 56, 59, 76, 77, 78, 129, 136, 162, 169, 171, 180
Birds 66, 68, 88, 95, 96
Black Notley 10, 73, 75
Blackmore 26, 27, 28, 61, 62, 112, 180
Blacksmith 25, 60
Blount, Elizabeth 26
Boleyn, Anne 26, 140, 141
Boniface V, Pope 25
Borley 123, 124, 125
Boreham 156, 181
Boudica 10, 176, 177
Bow Bridge 142, 166
Boy bishops 24
Bray, Margaret 54, 69
Bread 36, 45, 62, 76, 90, 97-9
Brentwood 25-6, 45, 53, 58, 66, 70, 76, 80, 82, 118-9, 127, 130-1, 140, 160-2, 164, 166, 173, 176, 180, 184
Bright, Edward 143
Brightlingsea 36, 68, 137
Broadside ballads 154
Brown, Arthur Henry 173
Bryan, Kate 160
Burghstead Lodge 136
Burnham-on-Crouch 144
Burns, Robert 50
Butler, Dr Cornelius 76
Buxton, Robert 100
Byrd, William 160, 172
Byrhtnoth 9, 136, 179, 180

Byron, Lord 164, 186
Caesar, Julius 72, 174
Cambridge Morris Men 168
Candlemas 50, 51
Canewdon 42, 43
Cater Museum 77
Chadwell Heath 120, 166
Chalkwell 64
Chapbooks 76, 154
Chapman, Michael 13
Charles II, King 23, 59, 94
Chaucer, Geoffrey 13
Cheese 88, 89
Chelmsford 10, 33, 34, 42, 45, 46, 48, 51, 54, 65, 99, 104, 113, 132, 135, 143, 145, 147, 152, 158, 163, 171, 176
Childerditch 84, 158
Chimney sweeps 60, 61
Chingford 94, 163
Christmas 8, 48, 51, 54, 69, 70, 71, 94, 96, 133, 170
Christy, Miller 85
Clarke, Mary 77
Claudius 175, 176, 177
Clavering 52, 99
Cobbett, William 103
Coggeshall 103, 138, 180
Coins 45, 46, 48, 108, 174
Colchester 10, 21-23, 36, 45-46, 54, 57, 68, 77, 79, 82, 88, 99, 100, 109, 114, 116, 118, 130, 134, 138, 142, 145, 152, 156, 174-178
Cole, Henry Sir 70
Constable, John 185
Copped Hall 95
Corn dollies 48, 49, 63
Crancher, Steve 152
Cromwell, Oliver 59
Culpeper, Nicholas 74
Dagenham 125, 152, 158
Danbury 114, 135
Dance 164-172
    Abbotts Bromley Horn 168
    Cambridge Morris 168
    Ceilidh, Grand Club 172
    Chingford Morris 163
    Cotswold Morris 169
    Headington 163
    Horn 168, 169
    Mayflower Morrismen 48, 56, 169, 171
    Scottish 172
    Thaxted Morris Men 168, 169

Day, Daniel 14
Day, James Wentworth 153
Deacon, Richard 39
De Bergh, Hubert 25, 26
Defoe, Daniel 65, 82, 89, 144
Dene Holes 121
Devil 118, 135, 166
Dickens, Charles 19
Dido 83, 84
Dineen, Frank 161
Dogs, Black 123
Doherty, Jimmy 97
Dovecotes 95
Dragons 56, 141
Dring, Fiddler 148
Dunmow Flitch 17, 18, 62, 88
Dunning, Edwin 186
Eales, Fred 59
East Horndon 140, 141, 142, 162
Eastbury House 66, 67
Easter 55, 58, 93, 130
Edward VI, King 32, 181
Elizabeth I, Queen 113, 164, 181
Ellis, Jon 53
Emmanuel church, Billericay 52, 54, 55
England, John 164
English Folk Dance and Song Society 160, 163, 164, 168, 171
Epiphany 48
Epping 135, 158, 181, 182
Erkenwald 178
Eryngo 100, 101
Essex Amateur Wine-making Association 101
Essex calf 94, 139
Essex Man 139, 153, 163
Essex pig 96, 97
Ethelburga 178
Fair, James 118, 119, 120
Fairlop Fair 21, 62, 88, 14, 19
Fairlop Oak 21
Fawkes, Guy 66, 67
Feering 9, 80
Felsted School 52
Finchingfield 120, 121
Fitzwalter, Sir Reginald 12
Ford Motor Co. 126, 127
Francis, Elizabeth 34, 35
Fry, Elizabeth 184
Fuller, Sarah 173
Gallows Corner 29, 127
George I, King 147
George II, King 182

Index

George III, King 100, 184
George IV, King 183
Gepp, Edward 152
Ghosts 41, 123, 128, 131, 136
Gidea Park 127, 158, 176
Good Easter Molly Men 48, 163, 171
Good Friday 53, 54
Goodchild, Robert 103
Great Bromley 35, 114
Great Burstead 57, 63, 112
Great Leighs 132
Great Warley 52, 53, 69, 103
Green Man 111, 112
Greensted 109
Gresham, Sir Thomas 181
Gunby, Norman 21, 141
Gutteridge, PC George 150
Gypsies 82
Hadleigh 40, 41, 146
Hainault 14, 83, 87, 93
Hall, Stephen 72
Halley, Elizabeth 91
Hallowe'en 66
Hancock, Chris 13
Harlow 51, 152, 173
Harold II, King 179
Harvest 34, 46, 48, 62, 63, 65, 96, 98, 161
Harwich 89, 100, 151, 164, 181
Hatfield Peverel 34, 36
Heatley, Revd 160
Henry Fitzroy 26, 27, 28
Henry I, King 142
Henry III, King 25, 93
Henry VII, King 165
Henry VIII, King 25, 31, 70, 181
Herbs 74, 75, 78, 84, 91, 101
Herrick, Robert 51
Hewett, Scrymgeour 89
Hockley 86, 87
Holst, Gustav 173
Hone's *Everyday Book*, 65
Hopkins, Matthew 39, 40
Hops 72, 78, 102, 103, 104
Hornchurch 70, 88, 110, 111
Horndon-on-the-Hill 54
Hot cross buns 53, 54
Huffers 99
Hunter, William 58, 130, 131
Ilford 21, 53, 166
Ingatestone 79, 88, 94, 103, 106, 107, 114, 115, 158, 181
Ingrave 58, 157, 160, 161, 162

Ireland, John 173
James I, King 37, 38, 94, 95
Jericho 27
John, King 25, 30, 133
Johnson, Dr Samuel 74, 144
Kelvedon 97, 112, 157, 176, 181
Kemp, Will 166, 167, 168
Kempe, Ursula 36
Kendall, Tony 163
Kennedy, Douglas 163
Kimber, William 163
King Cole 10
Kipling, Rudyard 72
Lady Day 55
Lady Jane Grey 181
Lammas 62, 63
Larkin, John 58
Leigh-on-Sea 90, 144
Lent 52, 53
Little Baddow 135
Little Burstead 162
London 178, 180, 182
Luther Stone 29, 30
Maiden's Garlands 110
Maldon 9, 21, 46, 47, 48, 92, 100, 104, 114, 130, 136, 143, 179, 180, 181
Manningtree 39, 144, 157
Maple, Eric 31, 43
Marconi, Guglielmo 10, 185
Marsh, Ken 126, 127
May Day 8, 56, 57, 58, 66
Mead 101
Mersea 21, 138, 146, 173
Michaelmas 23, 24, 65, 96
Mistley 39, 40
Monk, Dave 13, 16
Morant, Philip 27, 106, 111
Morgan, Glyn 34
Mordaunt, Lady 82
Morelli, Cesare 80, 82
Motley, Tony 168
Mountnessing 112, 157
Mumming Plays 170, 171
Murrell, James 40, 41
Music 114, 149, 160, 163, 171, 172, 173
New Year traditions 45
Noel, Conrad 168
Norden, John 88
Normans 8, 101
Northumberland, Duke of 181
Norwich 148, 166, 167
Nuclear bunker 122

Oak Apple Day 59
Occomore, David 155, 163
Oddy, Old 84
Owen, Peter 126
Oxenham, Mike 171
Oysters 21, 23, 46, 88
Paglesham 82, 122, 146
Paranormal Database 123, 128
Pearly King and Queen 149, 150
Peasants' Revolt 180
Peculiar People 184, 185
Pepys, Samuel 51, 64, 80, 82, 94, 164
Petre, Lord 184
Petre, Sir William 94, 181
Pewsey, Lynn 70, 87, 93
Phillips, Mary 40
Pickingill, George 42, 43
Pitt, Daniel 13, 16
Plants 8, 72, 73, 75, 91
Playford, John 171
Plough Monday 48, 49, 170
Paul VIII, Pope 33
Potiphar, Charles 161
Price, Harry 124, 125
Princess Margaret 172
Prittlewell 129, 144
Radio Caroline 149
Ray, John 10, 73, 74, 75, 80
Rayleigh 101, 130, 134, 146
Rayner, Claire 13, 16
Reddell, Jim 127
Riding Officers 145
Rochford 23, 24, 100, 141, 146, 156, 184
Rogationtide 58
Romans 8, 10, 21, 56, 72, 88, 97, 98, 101, 174, 176
Romford 85, 104, 125, 150, 158, 166, 169, 170
Royal Family 23
Rumford Morris Men 169
Runwell 117
Saffron 7, 80, 91, 92
Saffron Walden 25, 54, 75, 91, 114, 118, 141, 142, 148, 164, 173, 181
Salt 85, 99, 100, 159
Samphire 91, 92, 93
Scottish farmers 45
Scrapfaggot Green 132
Seaxes 9, 10
Shakespeare, William 92, 121, 141, 166, 174
Sharp, Cecil 160, 163, 164, 171, 172, 173
Shrovetide 52
Smuggling 122, 144, 145
Snakes 79

Southend 31, 54, 90, 91, 129, 134
South Weald 140, 164, 169, 186
St Cedd 178
St David's Day 53
St George's Day 56, 170
St Osyth 36, 37, 39, 113, 133, 179
St Peter on the Wall 178
St Thomas 173
St Valentine's Day 51, 52
Stearn, John 40
Stondon Massey 157, 172
Straw Jack 180
Stubbes, Philip 166
Superstitions 8, 9, 42, 44, 46, 63, 73, 91, 98, 113, 154, 159
Tallis, Thomas 172, 173
Taylor, Jane 173
Thaxted 168, 169, 173, 181
Theydon Mount 109, 135
Thomas, Richard 151
Thorpe-le-Soken 50, 67, 147
Thwaites, Simon 129
Tunbridge Wells 85
Turpin, Dick 182
Tyler, Wat 180
Tyrrells 140, 142, 156
Upminster (Tyler's) Common 28, 29, 30, 86, 87
Vange 87
Vaughan Williams, Dr Ralph 160, 161, 162, 163, 164
Vaughan, Eliza 78
Viper, The 79
Waltham Abbey 106, 172
Wanstead 100, 110, 181
Warley Barracks 84, 127, 128
Waterhouse, Joan 34, 35
Weald Hall 85, 140
Wheat-whoppers 61, 62
Whispering Court 23, 24
Whitebait Festival 90, 91
Whittier, John 79
Whybra, Julian 171
Wine-making 101
Witchcraft 8, 31, 32, 33, 34, 35, 36, 37, 38, 39, 40, 41, 42, 82
Woad 72
Woodham Ferrers 104, 181
Woolley, Hannah 78
Wormingford 56
Young, Arthur 97